KINGDOM MEDICINE

RELEASING CAPTIVES, RESTORING HEARTS
RAISING A HEALING ARMY

VOLUME 1

FOUNDATION FOR HEALING

ANGELA G. WALKER

KINGDOM MEDICINE 1: FOUNDATION FOR HEALING

Cover Artist: Rebecca Priestley
Cover Graphics: Caroline Bishop

ISBN 13: 9781656168115

ACKNOWLEDGEMENTS

Thank you to everyone who has provided valuable input and feedback in helping to shape the contents of this book, especially Guy Rothwell and David King. Also, thanks to Sue and Wendy for your contributions, and a special thanks to Rachel Gray for editing and proofreading the book.

A special thanks to Becky Priestley for her prophetic artwork (facebook.com/beckypriestleyy) and Caroline Bishop for her graphic designs on the cover.

Also, thank you dear friends and prayer warriors for your ongoing prayers and support throughout the writing of this book.

DEDICATION

I dedicate this book to the Great Physician, Jehovah-Rapha, from whom we receive spiritual insight and knowledge, wisdom and revelation, counsel and discernment, for every symptom, sickness and disease.

Thank you Heavenly Father, King Jesus and Holy Spirit, for teaching and demonstrating with such love and compassion, grace and mercy, power and authority, wisdom and revelation, how to heal the sick, set the captives free, release the prisoners from darkness, and heal the broken hearted. May all glory, power and honour be Yours, now and forever.

DISCLAIMERS

Kingdom Medicine does not seek to be in conflict with any medical or psychiatric practices, and values their contribution and input to healing and health care. It aims to work alongside them, by looking into the possible spiritual and emotional roots to symptoms, ill health and ongoing 'dis-ease'. Kingdom Medicine aims to connect the natural with the supernatural, and the physical with the emotional and spiritual.

Kingdom Medicine does not guarantee healing or prevention of symptoms. It facilitates healing and restoration between an individual and God. Hence, the fruits of this ministry will come forth out of the relationship between the person and God. It encourages people to be accountable to others (in the church and medical profession) for their ongoing physical, spiritual and emotional wellbeing.

Kingdom Medicine is not a substitute for medical advice or medical treatment. It aims to form a bridge between the medical health services and the Christian healing ministries.

Endorsement

As a medical doctor and a strong believer in the power of the Holy Spirit, Dr. Angela Walker is the perfect person to teach on Kingdom Medicine. Combining her knowledge from years of academic learning, experience in hands on medicine including on the mission fields of Africa, and her depth of faith, Angela brilliantly reveals the intertwined nature of the spirit, soul and body. Simply put, we can't expect fullness of health and the abundant life Jesus died to give us (John 10:10) if we are neglecting one of these areas.

In Volume 1 of Kingdom Medicine, Dr. Angela delves into areas such as spiritual history, hearing God's voice, faith, deliverance, and how one can be free of blockages to healing which may be missed if only the physical body is considered.

I highly recommend Dr. Angela's Manual which, when adhered to, can turn the tide of physical, emotional and spiritual health into the blessed life the Lord longs for us to live.

Patricia Bootsma
Catch the Fire Ministries
International Itinerant Speaker
Author of 'Convergence', 'Raising Burning Hearts', 'A Lifestyle of Divine Encounters'

CONTENTS

Introduction

Prayer

Foreword

Kingdom medicine is a wonderful resource for Health workers and Doctors especially those who follow Jesus Christ, but it is also a great resource those who may not, because it goes to the heart of many illnesses and diseases which are partially or wholly spiritual in origin. Spiritual problems need spiritual solutions for resolution! It gives spiritual principles to many human diseases and illnesses, which are barely touched upon in a western medical school education.

Dr Angela Walker is, I know from a personal friendship, a gifted and highly experienced Doctor and also a woman of great tenderness, humility and compassion.

What I love about this book is that she does not present Kingdom Medicine versus traditional Orthodox medicine as a one stop formula, or as another proposition, but as a valuable and often essential adjunct to our normal medical practice. She freely admits in the book to receiving conventional treatment in a London Hospital for a bout of malaria she contracted in South Sudan.

A deep sense of caring and concern runs throughout the book and she freely admits that a strong sense of compassion is essential along with faith to see the outworking of the miraculous.

Kingdom medicine is balanced and comprehensive, giving blockages to healing, loving advice as to how to develop a healing ministry, along with important principles for wholeness.

I highly recommend this well researched and well written book as a valuable aid to all who are involved in the caring professions.

Dr Martin Panter

MBBS, MRCS, DTM&H, FRACGP, FRSTM, FACTM
Founder & Chairman of HART (Humanitarian Aid Relief Trust)

Introduction

At the time of releasing this book, the nations were in the middle of a global pandemic crisis caused by the Corona virus, known as *Covid 19*. This virus was rapidly spreading across the nations, causing governments to shutdown schools, businesses, industries, social gatherings (such as, restaurants, pubs, entertainment and sports venues), and churches. Even flights were grounded as the nations were forced to close their borders. Amongst the frontline workers were the healthcare services and military forces, as they fought to save lives, heal the sick and provide protection for the communities. These people were willing to risk their own lives as they put the lives of others before themselves. Together, they formed a 'healing army'.

Around ten years ago, the Lord spoke through a vision. In this vision, I was on board a white ship named H.M.S or 'His Majesty's Service'. This was no ordinary ship but a royal military ship and the Captain was King Jesus. It was a royal ship, because those who served were sons and daughters of the King. It was a military ship because the crew were empowered and equipped to rescue captives, free prisoners, quench fears, and overcome the lies of the enemy. Essentially, this ship was a training base for those who were willing to lay down their lives for the King, as they signed up to serve Him, in His healing army.

As I was taken around the ship, I was led to a cabin room. This was a spotless, clean white room, and I suddenly realized it was an operating room. In the centre was an operating table. Next, in walked the Great Surgeon, Jesus Himself. I asked Him what operation was He doing, and He replied, 'Open heart surgery'. The vision ended.

Jesus is our Jehovah Rapha, the Lord who heals (Exodus 15:26), and Jehovah Sabaoth, the Lord of hosts (or Commander of the armies of the Lord). This is because He heals the sick, restores lives, heals hearts, frees prisoners, rescues captives, raises the dead and protects us from the enemy (Exodus 12:12-13, Revelation 12:11, Psalm 91:1-16). Kingdom Medicine is about restoring hearts, releasing captives and raising a healing army, as we turn to King Jesus for our healing, inner freedom and divine protection.

After seven years of doing medical missions with Iris Ministries (now Iris Global), I started to explore the healing tools in other ministries. The combination of these spiritual tools along with personal experiences, spiritual and medical insights has become 'Kingdom Medicine'. Kingdom Medicine combines the supernatural with the natural, and the physical with the spiritual and emotional, by co-labouring with the Great Physician, Jesus. During my medical career as a Paediatrician (that is, children's doctor), my work involved 'Child Health and development'. The Lord has transformed my natural work into a supernatural ministry of 'Divine Health and Spiritual Development'.

Health is not just about our body being in good shape; health also encompasses our heart, mind and spirit. What goes on in our heart, mind and spirit has effect on our body and vice versa. Each has influence over the other. The Lord created us so we could have the capacity to worship and love Him with *all* our soul, *all* our heart, *all* our mind and *all* our strength. In other words, every part of our being is to worship God and love Him. He created us to live, breathe and move in harmony and unity with the Father, Son and Holy Spirit.

Spiritual growth and development, involves nurturing God's children from born-again babies to little children to mature sons and daughters, through the process of divine sonship and healing. Spiritual sonship refers to our relationship with God as His sons and daughters. Hence, Kingdom Medicine is about healing the sick, setting the captives free, transforming hearts, and empowering God's sons and daughters to walk in their royal identity and spiritual authority. Spiritual nurturing is vital in the body of Christ, so we may discover the ways and heart of God, and mature in our spiritual identity and authority.

Somewhere in our life, 'negative' experiences and ungodly influences have hindered or blocked our relationship with God and one another. These include generational sins and curses, childhood bullying or abuse, abandonment and rejection, self-hate or resentment, false beliefs about God and ourselves, occult influences and new age practices, hurts and wounds, fears and lies.

Whether we are aware of it or not, these negative influences have caused us to be in some degree of emotional, physical and spiritual bondage. Kingdom Medicine aims to open eyes, unblock ears, strengthen limbs, and decree freedom to the body, soul and spirit. This is to enable God's sons and daughters to see in the Spirit, hear in the Spirit and move in the Spirit, fulfilling their divine calling and purpose.

Volume One helps provide a *Foundation For Healing* that is based on our intimacy with God. Our intimate relationship with God helps us to develop further in the areas of healing and freedom, both individually and corporately. The foundation includes hearing God, taking a spiritual history, spiritual roots to sickness and disease, understanding the spirit, soul and body, spiritual strongholds and deliverance guidelines. The truth is we are all called to heal the sick and set the captives free as part of our daily lifestyle. This book aims to encourage and equip the body of Christ to minister to one another in the area of healing, so healing becomes the norm in everyone's life. Supernatural healing is to flow out of our intimate relationship with God.

Volume Two provides *Kingdom Tools* used in the various areas of healing. Just as there are various departments in a hospital, so there are various tools to minister in the different areas of healing. Having a foundation helps to use these tools with greater efficacy, and use them not by might, nor by strength but by the power of His Spirit working through us (Zechariah 4:6).

Volume Three provides additional tools for the purpose of *Divine Heart Surgery.* Divine Heart Surgery is a deeper ministry that involves assisting the Great Surgeon as He operates on the hearts of His people. As we minister in His presence, we have the privilege of being led by His Spirit, as He delicately heals the wounded and traumatized areas of the heart.

I am an ongoing learner with a passion to see God's children healed, set free, restored, and nurtured into their fullness of maturity as His sons and daughters. The Lord is continually revealing new things, as we choose to press on deeper in our intimacy with Him.

Healing is both to receive and to give away. Jesus commissioned His disciples to; *'Heal the sick, raise the dead, cleanse the lepers, drive out demons. Freely you have received, freely give,'* (Matthew 10:8). Our spiritual journey is one of continual nurturing through the healing of hearts and transforming of minds, as we hunger for more of His presence.

Heidi Baker gave this prophetic word many years ago at a church in Singapore, but I believe it is still relevant for our churches today: *'The Lord said, "There is a lot of infection in the church that causes her not to run and I want to heal My church and close her wounds. But if I am to heal My church and close her wounds then she needs to understand who she is. She is created as a resting place for Me. She is to finish well... she is created to carry My glory". Who will become a resting place for Him?'*

Sadly, there is much physical and spiritual 'dis-ease' in the body of Christ today. Hence, the Lord wants to cleanse and restore His body, especially the wounded areas of our hearts, so we can grow deeper in fellowship with Him, discover who we are, and create a place in our hearts for His Spirit to come and rest.

May the Lord equip and empower you to heal the sick, raise the dead, set the captives free and heal the broken-hearted - not by might, nor by power but by His Spirit dwelling in you (Zechariah 4:6, Isaiah 61:1). I believe we are all called to practice Kingdom Medicine, especially for such a time as this.

Prayer

Here is a prayer I say regularly and especially before ministering to others. I believe it is powerful and protects from the influences of the evil one. Over time, we can develop our own prayers as we are led by the Spirit to pray.

The prayer aligns our spirit to come under the influence of God, sanctifies our whole being, filters what we allow in and out, opens our five senses to the Holy Spirit and welcomes the seven-fold Spirit to teach, counsel and guide. I have subdivided it for the purpose of outlining these areas in the prayer. This is the prayer:

Alignment with Spirit of God
Lord, I surrender my body, soul and spirit to You. I command my flesh (body and soul) to come under my spirit and my spirit to come under the influence of Your Holy Spirit. Holy Spirit guide me in all my thoughts, choices and actions (mind, will and emotions).

Sanctify Mind, Heart & Spirit
Lord, cleanse and sanctify my mind, will, emotions, spirit and imagination with Your blood. I command any negative or unclean thoughts to leave in Jesus' Name, including any unclean spirits picked up from conversations, social media or other sources. I wash them off and by faith receive cleansing through the power of Your blood (1 Thessalonians 5:23: sanctify body, soul and spirit).

Divine Filter *(for what you allow in and out)*
Lord, filter what I hear and see and what I release through my thoughts and words. Prevent me from receiving or saying anything not of You, through the power and protective covering of Your blood (Ezekiel 44).

Welcome Seven fold Spirit of God *(Is 11:2, Ephesians 1)*
I welcome Your Presence and the Spirit of Wisdom, Revelation (Truth &
Understanding), Knowledge, Fear of Lord, Counsel and Power, to guide
me in all I see, think and do. Thank you Lord, I can do nothing without
Your grace, so I lean on You to teach and instruct me the ways to go.

Open Eyes, Ears and Senses
Lord, increase my spiritual senses. Open my eyes to see, my ears to hear,
my nose to sniff out and discern, and my senses to feel things in the
Spirit. Increase my hunger to know You more and transform my mind
and heart as I daily rest in Your presence (Hebrews 5:14)

1

Divine Healing & Sonship

Jesus went throughout Galilee, preaching the Good News of the
Kingdom, and healing every disease and sickness among the people

Matthew 4:23

Kingdom Medicine is about healing the spirit, soul and body by
co-labouring with the Great Physician, Jesus. After many years
working as a hospital children's doctor, the Lord called me to the
mission field, where He taught me how to heal the sick, His way.
(More can be read in: *'From Natural to Supernatural, Healing God's
Way'*). Since then, I have been on a journey of discovering various
tools and ways to minister alongside the Holy Spirit in different
areas of healing. Receiving healing is not the end-point. The whole
purpose of the healing ministry is to draw us closer to God. The
qualifications for this ministry are not found in man-made
certificates, but rather in the qualifications of the heart. As we
grow deeper in intimacy with God, we will receive more
compassion and anointing. Compassion helps to release healing,
and we receive compassion through a broken, contrite heart.

God calls us to co-labour *with* Him. Many of us are doing
things for Him or expect Him to bless us as we minister to others.
However, He wants us to do things with Him. He is wooing us to
be with Him, dance with Him, laugh with Him, share in His

17

suffering love and abide in Him. His glory-presence starts to flow as we choose to rest in Him and let His Spirit dwell in us (John 15:4-5). All of this comes from choosing a lifestyle of pursuing His presence.

Spiritual Paediatrics

One day, I felt the Lord impress on my heart that He was going to teach me 'spiritual paediatrics'. He revealed that in His Kingdom, children range from newborn babies to adults of over one hundred years of age. There is no age limit to spiritual paediatrics because we are all God's children, and we all need healing from something or another. Most of us require healing from a physical illness or injury, as well as emotional pain such as rejection, fear, and trauma from our adult or childhood experiences. Hence, spiritual paediatrics is about healing God's children, not only in body but also in soul and spirit.

As a children's doctor I was involved in two areas known collectively as *'Child Health and Development'*. In spiritual terms, health is all about healing our body, soul and spirit, whereas, development is about our spiritual growth. Hence, the Lord revealed something simple yet profound, how healing and nurturing go together.

Spiritual Growth & Maturing in Sonship

Many of us may have the gifts of the Spirit (as Paul speaks of in 1 Corinthians 12), but they do not mean we are any more mature or closer in our relationship with God. They do not reflect our level of spiritual growth or intimacy with God. This is because they are given freely by the grace of God. We have done nothing to earn or deserve them, so we have no room to boast. We usually receive the gifts whilst we are immature and young in our faith, because they are to help us encourage and build up one another.

Another thing I've come to realize is God isn't bothered about our abilities. In fact, they can become a stumbling block if we rely on them more than Him. When we do things in our own strength and abilities, we tend to look for praise and recognition for what we have done. This can lead to pride because we like to boast about what we have achieved or done (1 John 2:16). Since all our abilities, natural and supernatural, are given to us by God, then we have no room to boast. I believe God wants us to rely more on His Spirit, instead of relying on our self (Roman 11:17-18).

God is more interested in our character and attitude, than our gifts. The degree that we live by the *fruit* of His Spirit reflects our maturity in relationship with Him. The closer we become to someone, the more influence the person has. The same is true when we hang out in God's presence. As we choose to soak in His presence by spending time with Him, He will gently mould us like clay in a potter's hand, and we will become more like Him.

Healing plays a major role in our spiritual growth and development. The Lord is passionate about healing His sons and daughters. He longs to set us free from captivity so we may grow in intimacy with Him, and fulfill His amazing purpose and calling. Once people become healed and set free, they are then in a position to help others find healing and freedom.

Spiritual growth is about developing in sonship as we grow from new born babies to young *[teknon]* sons and from young sons to mature *[huios]* sons, and ultimately to become Christ's mature bride. In English, we have only one word for 'son'. However, in the New Testament there are different Greek words used for 'son'. The Greek word *tecknon*[2] is used to refer to the little child or spiritually immature son (1 John 3:10, Romans 8:16-17). Paul referred to Timothy as his *tecknon* son (2 Timothy 2:1). In comparison, the Greek word *huios*[3] is used to refer to the spiritually mature son or the son who is developed in character. God referred to Jesus as His [huios] Son (Matthew 3:17). Also, Paul spoke of the manifestation of the mature [huios] sons of God that were to be revealed (Romans 8:19).

Spiritual maturity has nothing to do with how long we have been a Christian, or about gaining qualifications or attending Bible College. Rather, it's about the depth of our intimate relationship with God. God designed us so we could experientially know Him. This means experiencing God in our hearts as our Father and Judge, Jesus as our Brother, Lord and

Bridegroom King, and the Holy Spirit as our Counselor, Nurturer and Companion. We can ask Father God to show us where we are in our spiritual growth, and we shouldn't be surprised if He reveals we are a toddler or little son and daughter. The truth is most of us may think we are mature Christians, when we are probably just scraping the surface. There is far more to discover in His Kingdom that will blow our minds.

The Lord wants to heal our hearts and call us into deeper communion with Him. Spiritual sonship involves developing in the areas of *Belonging, Identity, the Suffering Heart of Christ* and *Anointing.* (For more on this read, *'Into His Chambers'*[4]).

We are all on a spiritual journey, and as we allow His Spirit to guide and counsel us through life, we will experience inner healing, enjoy deeper intimacy, and grow in spiritual maturity. Spiritual maturity is about developing our character and growing in our God-given authority, as well as taking on our royal identity. In order to develop from His little children to His mature sons and daughters, we need to constantly hunger for more of His presence by making Him our first love.

Three things are essential if we want to continue to run the race God has marked out for us (Hebrews 12:1). First, we need a *hunger* in our hearts for more of His presence. Second, we need to daily *surrender* our hearts to Him. And third, we need to learn to *rest in His presence.* All of these are about pursuing a life of abiding in Him. The more we allow Him to cleanse and transform various areas in our hearts, the greater the capacity we have to love others and become carriers of His presence.

Spiritual Dwellings

God created us to be spiritual houses or spiritual dwellings, and just as a house has many rooms, including a basement and attic, so we have many rooms or areas in our heart. Paul said: *'And in Him you too are being built together to become a dwelling in which God lives by His Spirit,'* (Ephesians 2:22, 1 Corinthians 3:16). Our spiritual dwelling is our innermost being. In our innermost being, there may be some 'protected' areas and 'dark' rooms. These may be the result of hidden wounds, shame or sins. These rooms appear dark because the light of Jesus doesn't dwell in them, and they are protected because of the defense barriers we have put up over time to protect our hurt emotions.

In one area of our heart, we may be able to worship and connect to God's Spirit, but other areas may be blocked or closed to His Spirit. It's like a home having a light turned on in the kitchen, but the other rooms are closed or full of darkness. If we want to experience more of His presence, then we need to deal with our sins and wounds. Once we receive the necessary cleansing and healing, then He can come and occupy these areas in our hearts (Matthew 23:25). We simply need to invite Him in, as we give Him permission to cleanse and heal each area of our heart. *'The lamp of the Lord searches the spirit of a man; it searches out his inmost being'* (Proverbs 20:27). *'If your heart is open to hear My voice and you open the door within, I will come into you and feast with you and you will feast with Me,'* (TPT Revelation 3:20).

Dr Luke

Luke was a first-century Gentile and a Doctor who wrote about the healings and miracles of Jesus in the Gospel of Luke and the Book of Acts. What happened in the Book of Acts is available for us now, and more, because Jesus said we would do greater things than He did then (John 14:12). One of the best ways to witness to people about Jesus is through healing. A common false belief concerning ministering healing to others is this: 'What if they don't get healed when I pray?...I'd better not risk it.' The truth is we are not the ones who do the healing. God is the One who heals! We become His vessels or conduits as we simply connect His Spirit to others through prayer. The result is up to Him. It changes everything when we start thinking like this. God will use anyone, even a little child, to heal someone. He longs for the lost to know Him, for the stray to come home and the wounded to receive healing. He is looking for those who will be a vessel of His love and release His salvation, healing and deliverance. It is not about how great we are, but how great He is!

I have seen people fully healed on the spot, or in part or not healed at all. However, in some cases when I have seen no healing, I have heard they were healed hours later or the next morning. Sometimes, there may be reasons why someone isn't healed, and other times there is no explanation. I believe we should pray for healing, because if we don't then we won't see it. If we are not prepared to be a labourer in His harvest, then we can't expect to see results. There is nothing to lose but everything to gain. Healing is not just for the qualified doctor or pastor, but for each one of us. There is a great need for labourers in God's Kingdom. Hence, we should train and release His people in this end-time harvest. It is both exciting and an adventure when you start reaching out and see God's power move in people's lives. And the more you reach out, the more you will see, for the Lord will increase His anointing on His faithful ones.

Corporate Healings

Sometimes, there isn't enough time to minister one to one, hence, there needs to be more opportunities for the corporate healing of hearts. Corporate healing can occur in small groups, at conferences or church gatherings. At such gatherings, the spiritual atmosphere can be prepared through prayer and worship, as we come together and engage in His presence. When we are in the presence of the Lord, then the Lord may come and minister to the hearts of His people.

Heart of Sonship

God wants to transform our minds and hearts from an orphan heart and mindset to one of sonship. This means no longer having an independent, self-sufficient, selfish, anxious or ambitious spirit, but instead one of complete trust and dependency on Him. It means learning how to live in the power and grace of His Spirit on a daily basis. Our Father likes laughing with us and enjoys being with us. He invites us to hold His hand and journey through life with Him. He will never leave or abandon us, for His Spirit is always with us. He has given us free will to do what we choose but if we leave Him, He patiently waits for us to return. His Master plan is written in the Book of Life for you and me. '*All the days ordained for me were written in Your book before one of them came to be'* (Psalm 139:16). He knows our future and what lies ahead, hence has the best plans for us. *'For I know the plans I have for you, plans to prosper you and not to harm you, plans to give you a hope and a future... You will seek Me and find Me, **when you seek Me with all your heart'*** (Jeremiah 29:11). Though we may fail Him, His love for us will never fail. His main desire is that we seek His presence, not with one percent but with *all* of our heart.

When Jesus stepped into His long awaited ministry, He read from the scroll: *'The Spirit of the Lord is upon Me, and He has anointed Me to bring Good News for the poor, freedom for the broken-hearted and new eyes for the blind and to preach to the prisoners, 'You are set free!' I have come to share the message of Jubilee, for the time of God's great acceptance has begun,'* (Luke 4:18-20, The Passion Translation. See Isaiah 61:1-3). Jesus not only came to bring physical healing, but to rescue us from spiritual bondage. He wants to open our eyes to see Him and our ears to hear Him as we enter in deeper communion with Him. Our Heavenly Father sent His One and only Son to rescue us from captivity and bring us back into this intimate love relationship with Him.

I was in a good relationship (or so I thought) with the Lord whilst serving Him on the mission field with Iris Ministries in Africa. However, during a season of transition, He started to do deeper work in my heart. As I kept surrendering the various areas of my carnal nature to Him, I became aware of an increase in His presence resting in me. It was as if my life was slowly transforming from a caterpillar into a butterfly. The life of a butterfly is about moving in His Spirit, and realizing that it is no longer I who live but Christ who lives in me (Galatians 2:20). This is a Spirit-led life as we choose to go where He goes and do what we see Him doing. Our life is no longer our own, but belongs to Him!

Many have remained crippled, wounded or stunted in their spiritual growth through insufficient or incorrect nutrition. Our spiritual nutrition involves growing in His Word and Spirit, as we seek more of His presence. We continue to grow through dealing with our wounds and negative beliefs in our hearts. The Lord is passionate to heal and cleanse us from all ungodly thoughts, so we can radiate His love in His Kingdom. This process of transformation from caterpillars into beautiful butterflies involves undergoing 'auto-digestion' or 'death to self', where we surrender the areas of our carnal nature to Him.

One day the Lord spoke to me through a picture of a bowl full of white, finely refined flour. I wondered why the Lord gave me this picture and this is what I wrote: *'Flour is refined and purified from grains of wheat that have been broken and crushed. However, the yeast of the Spirit needs to be added so it may rise. I am raising you up. You are not to be 'self-raising flour' but to wait for Me to raise you up. As you carry My presence and anointing, you will offer My bread, My Living Word, which will bring healing, life and freedom to those who receive. I am the Bread of Life. He who eats My flesh and drinks My blood will have eternal life. My Word carries Truth and will set the captives free. As you remain broken and poured out for Me, as a daily offering of yourself, I will raise you up and use you to feed and heal My people. So do not become 'self-raising' flour, but abide in Me and let My Spirit raise you up to feed My people!'* (See also John 6:39-40). I believe this word applies to us all.

The Lord wants us to learn how to live not by might nor by strength but by His Spirit. This means living by His Spirit of Wisdom and Revelation, Counsel and Might, Knowledge and the Fear of the Lord, as we pursue a life of resting in His presence. '**The Spirit of the Lord will rest** on Him- the **Spirit of wisdom** and of **understanding, the Spirit of counsel** and of **power**, the **Spirit of knowledge** and of **the fear of the Lord'** (Isaiah 11:2). These spiritual qualities are more than the gifts referred to in 1 Corinthians 12. A gift is a miniscule portion of the Spirit. The gifts of wisdom and knowledge are described as a *word* of knowledge and a *word* of wisdom (1 Corinthians 12:8). This is tiny compared to the *Spirit* of wisdom and the *Spirit* of knowledge. Jesus didn't operate from the gifts of the Spirit for He was God incarnate, the Word made flesh. The Spirit of the Lord was in and upon Him. Likewise, the Lord desires to make His home in us, for He wants His Spirit to come and dwell in us, so we are fully in Him and He is fully in us (John 14:23). Jesus is Wisdom personified and as we dwell in His presence, He will reveal His Wisdom, Knowledge, Revelation and Counsel (1 Corinthians 1:30, Proverbs 8:1-14).

Intimacy with God is essential if we want to minister to others in the power of His Spirit. It is my prayer that as the Lord operates on our hearts, we may grow deeper in love with Him.

Less of our flesh means more room for His presence. Greater anointing flows from the place of abiding in His presence.

END NOTES

[1] Dr Walker, Angela; *From Natural to Supernatural, Healing God's Way, (2014)*

[2] Teknon (Greek 5043); *Strong's Expanded Exhausted Concordance: Red Letter Edition, (2001)*

[3] Huios (Greek 5207); *Strong's Expanded Exhausted Concordance: Red Letter Edition, (2001)*

[4] Dr Walker, Angela; *Into His Chambers, (2018)*

2

Jehovah Rapha

I will not bring on you any of the diseases I brought on the Egyptians,
for I am the Lord who heals you

Exodus 15:26

One of the Lord's names is *Jehovah Rapha*, the **Lord who heals**. I believe the reason God wants to heal is to draw us closer to Him. God wants to heal not just our physical sickness or disabilities, but the areas of bondage in our heart. Different parts of our emotions may be trapped in time and space, as a result of childhood trauma. However, these wounded emotions can receive healing when presented to Jesus. We all need healing from hurts and freeing from bondage of one sort or another, since negative emotions or experiences occur in life.

There can be various roots to sickness and disease, and these may be the results of sins or curses, including the sins of our forefathers. Sin provides an opportunity for the enemy to inflict sickness and draw us into bondage (Deuteronomy 28:1-15). Since Jesus was without sin, He had no sickness or disease. He was never in bondage for the devil had no *hold* on Him (John 14:30). Jesus mentioned how the unrepentant people would be filled with the *sins of their forefathers* (Matthew 23:32).

27

It is so easy to open ourselves to demonic influence and not be aware, especially when watching films, TV and adverts, reading books, or through social media and the internet. Likewise, we may expose ourselves to ungodly spirits when we visit alternative therapists such as those who practice homeopathy, acupuncture, reiki, reflexology, and so on. (For more information on this, see chapter on 'Alternative Medicines' in Volume Two of Kingdom Medicine).

God heals ALL sickness and diseases (Psalm 103:3). There is nothing He can't heal for He is our Creator. He made us in His image. When Jesus went around preaching the Good News, He also healed every sickness and disease amongst those who were brought to Him (Matthew 4:23). Everyone who came for healing, whether epileptic, paralyzed or demon-possessed, He healed and set free! Even the dead He raised back to life. Since Jesus was without sin, He had the power and authority over every sickness, disease and even death itself. One of His leaving comments was this: *'I tell you the truth, anyone who has faith in Me will do what I have been doing. He will do even greater things than these because I am going to the Father,'* (John 14:12).

The Lord will call some to minister to the outcasts of society including the addicts, the homeless, those in satanic or occult activity, or those in the sex trade industry. Who will go? Who will say, 'Here am I Lord, send me!' By God healing our hearts and taking us deeper in union with Him, we can become like a fragrant love offering to those around us.

How Did Jesus Heal?

One way of learning how to heal the sick is to look at how Jesus and His disciples healed. Jesus healed physically, emotionally and spiritually, if not all at once. Many times, the sick received healing after He addressed an area of unforgiveness, or freed a person from demonic spirits. So let's start by looking in the scriptures at the tools Jesus used to heal the sick. Also, note that what Jesus did was simply a reflection of His relationship of Sonship with His Father.

Prayer & Fasting

Jesus prayed and fasted for forty days before He stepped into His long awaited ministry. Fasting is part of the healing ministry. Jesus let His disciples experiment on healing the sick. On one occasion, they were unable to cast a spirit out of a boy who was fitting. Jesus said it was because of their lack of faith, and this evil spirit would only come out with prayer *and fasting* (Mathew 17:19-21). Fasting is a whole subject in itself, but it is one of the spiritual disciplines where our flesh submits to our spirit, and God empowers our spirit as we yield to Him (see Chapter 12 *'When You Fast'*).

There are satanists who fast for 'spiritual breakthrough' to bring division, destruction and death to the body of Christ. If satanists receive an increase in demonic power through fasting, think how powerful it is when Christians fast and God releases His warring angels to bring Kingdom breakthrough (see Daniel 10:2-14).

Jesus taught us to pray: *'Your Kingdom come, Your will be done, on earth as it is in Heaven'* (Matthew 6:10). Remember there is no sickness or disease in heaven. If we want to serve God doing Kingdom ministry then I believe our lives must be one of prayer along with fasting. Then we can powerfully pray, *'Your Kingdom come and will be done, on earth as in heaven'*.

Anointing & Power

Jesus' time in the wilderness was a season of preparation. He entered the desert *filled with the Holy Spirit,* but returned to Galilee and started His ministry *in the power of the Spirit* (Luke 4:14). God anointed Jesus with the Holy Spirit and power, and He healed all who were under the power of the devil, *because God was with Him* (Acts 10:38).

Jesus fulfilled what was written in Isaiah 61: *'The Spirit of the Lord is on Me, because the Lord has anointed Me...'* The Spirit of God that rested upon Jesus anointed Him to minister to the sick. This is not the gift of healing. Rather, it is the sevenfold Spirit mentioned in Isaiah, including the *Spirit of the Lord, Wisdom, Understanding, Knowledge, Counsel, Power* and *the Fear of the Lord* (Isaiah 11:1-3).

It is good to be aware of the anointing we carry. Some may have anointing for certain areas of healing. However, we need wisdom and discernment when to minister to someone or when not to, and when to refer to others. Sometimes, God may call us to step in an area we haven't ministered in before. As long as we lean on Him and rely on His Spirit, we will discover many things in His Kingdom.

Authority

Jesus had authority over all sicknesses and demonic spirits. His authority came from His intimate relationship with the Father, because He always submitted to the will of His Father (John 5:19-27). He demonstrated His authority to the paralytic man by saying: *'So that you may know that the Son of Man has authority on earth to forgive sins.... get up, take your mat and go home'*, and the man did likewise (Matthew 9:6). His authority was noted when He commanded the sickness or demon(s) to go, and people were healed. What He declared came into being for there was authority in His words (Matthew 7:29). The sickness or demons had to submit to His authority. Likewise, we have the same authority in what we speak or pray, through the power of His Spirit dwelling in us.

Faith & Action

Jesus had faith. He could see what His Father was doing and followed His will constantly. Our faith should be such that we take action and do as we hear or see our Father doing in Heaven. Faith is released as we engage our spirit with God, and declare what we see Him doing, releasing it on earth as we see it taking place in Heaven. Faith is knowing what is on God's heart for others and agreeing in the Spirit even before we see it happening on earth.

Sometimes, the Lord gives us promptings to do simple prophetic acts, like testing the part of the body that needs healing. He told the cripple to stretch out his hand and as he did his arm was healed. Healing is released when we *step out* in faith. This is where action follows faith. Jesus told the paralytic to *get up, take up his mat and walk*. As he did, he was healed (Mark 2:11). It was after the blind man went and *washed his eyes in the pool* that he came back seeing (John 9:7). Jesus instructed the lepers to go and see the priests and *as they went,* they were healed (Luke 17:14). When healing a man who was both deaf and mute, Jesus put His *fingers in the man's ears* and then *spat and touched his tongue.* After this, He then looked up to Heaven and commanded, 'Be opened!' (Mark 7:33).

Laying on of Hands

'*When the sun was setting, the people brought to Jesus all who had various kinds of sickness, and laying His hands on each one, He healed them'*(Luke 4:40). Those whom Jesus laid hands on were healed.

On one occasion, Jesus had to pray more than once for a person. He prayed and *laid hands twice* on a blind man's eyes before He received normal vision (Mark 8:25). Jesus spoke healing over the crippled woman *then He put His hands on her* and she immediately straightened her back (Luke 13:13).

Some Christians fear touching others who have contagious diseases or carry demons for concern they'll get it too. This was also the mindset of the Israelites. The man with leprosy cried out on his knees begging Jesus saying: *'Lord, if You are willing, You can make me clean'.* Jesus' reply was to first reach out and touch the man. Then He said: '*I am willing, be clean'* (Mark 1:40-41, Mathew 8:2-3). I believe Jesus touched the man first as a demonstration of His love and compassion to heal someone who was unclean. Jesus did not fear coming into physical contact with this contagious disease (or skin infested disease), for His power and authority were greater than the sickness or disease.

Touch or the laying on of hands releases healing. Likewise, faith followed by action releases healing. However, we must be sensitive to only touch an acceptable part of the person's body, such as hold their hand or ask permission if it involves touching their arm or leg. Or if it is the abdomen we can get them to lay hands over the area and then lay our hands gently on top of their hands. We should avoid touching private areas or forcing our hands on the head. Rather, respect their body and be gracious to them. This includes being sensitive to those who have been abused, for in such cases it may not be appropriate to touch. Sometimes, all that is required is to look into the person's eyes.

When we look in the eyes, we minister directly to their spirit, for the eyes are the gateway to the heart (Matthew 6:22).

Forgiveness of Sins

Jesus demonstrated healing through the *forgiveness of sins.* He forgave the sins of the paralytic man. He said: *'Son, your sins are forgiven'* (Mark 2:3-12). Then the man got up, took his mat and walked.

In another incidence, Jesus went up to a man who had been crippled for thirty-eight years and was lying by a pool. Jesus asked: *'Do you want to get well?'* This may seem a strange thing to ask, but some don't want to be healed! Their sickness is their identity and income. Or they may want healing but are not willing to deal with the roots behind their symptoms. Jesus later found the same man he had healed at the temple and said: *'Stop sinning or something worse may happen to you,'* (John 5:1-14). Jesus had healed him but the man may have been unaware his sickness was the result of sin.

'Praise the Lord, who **forgives** *all your sins* **and heals** *all your diseases'* (Psalm 103:3). In the Old Testament, forgiveness was known to release physical healing. The Lord said to His people that if they listened to Him and did what was right in His eyes, obeying His commands, then no sickness or disease would fall on them (Exodus 15:26).

Compassion

Jesus had compassion on *all* He healed. *'Jesus went through all the towns and villages, teaching in the synagogues, preaching the good news of the Kingdom and* **healing every disease and sickness**. *When He saw the crowds,* **He had compassion on them**' (Mathew 9:35, 14:14 & 20:34). Filled with compassion, Jesus reached out His hand, touched the man with leprosy and said, 'Be clean!' (Mark 1:41). The word leprosy was commonly used when referring to an unclean skin disease. Hence, to touch a man with 'leprosy' was an act of love and compassion. Com-passion is reaching out to people 'with love' or 'with fiery passion'. Jesus wasn't afraid of encountering demonic spirits; they were afraid of Him and what He was going to do with them. Compassion releases healing.

Binding & Loosening

Jesus instructed demonic spirits to, *'Be quiet!'* and then commanded them to leave the person by saying, *'Come out of him!'* (Mark 1:25). This is binding and casting out demons. Jesus spoke few words, but because His words carried authority, they were powerful and effective. We too can command any manifesting spirit or demon to be quiet and stop manifesting, before ordering it to leave the person's body in Jesus' Name. As already mentioned, it's not about how many words we say, it's about the spiritual authority we carry. We also need to be aware of what we are dealing with as sometimes we may need to approach the situation differently.

Jesus spoke to Peter and gave him the keys of the Kingdom of Heaven, to bind and loosen, on earth as it is in Heaven. That is to bind on earth what has already been bound in Heaven and to loosen on earth what has already been loosened in Heaven (Matthew 16:19). Jesus later repeated this message to a wider audience: *'I tell you the truth, whatever you bind on earth will be bound in heaven, and whatever you loose on earth will be loosed in heaven'* (Matthew 18:18). We know there is no sickness or disease in Heaven, hence we can bind sickness on earth and loosen healing, as we see it is in Heaven. That is why we pray: *'Your Kingdom come Your will be done, on earth as in heaven'*.

Jesus addressed the evil spirit(s) by referring to the function it did. In one person, He commanded a deaf and mute spirit to leave, and in another, He cast out a spirit of infirmity: *'**You deaf and mute spirit**. I command you, come out of him and never enter him again'*(Mark 9:25). He spoke differently to the crippled woman: *'A woman was there who had been **crippled by a spirit** for eighteen years. She was bent over and could not straighten up at all. Jesus said, "Woman, you are **set free from your infirmity**"'* (Luke 13:11-13).

I don't believe it is necessary to speak to demons to find out who they are before commanding them out of individuals. This is only giving them unnecessary attention. We can always rely on the Holy Spirit to give us the knowledge and discernment we need when setting someone free from an evil spirit. When we sense there could be an evil spirit behind someone's illness, we simply bind the spirit behind the symptoms, and command it to leave in Jesus' Name. This is fine if the person is in agreement with what we are praying. However, if the person isn't in agreement or is not yet a Spirit-filled believer, then they may start to manifest because the demon is resisting deliverance. If this should happen, it is wise to first bind the demon, and then ask the person to invite Jesus into their heart. Now get the person to take authority and renounce the demon, and when they tell it to go, it has to go.

Some cases may require a different method of ministry to deal with the spirit(s) behind the sickness. Another way to receive healing and freedom is through worshipping in the glory-presence. Demons hate the presence of God and hence have to leave when a person is worshipping in the Spirit and presence of God. The demons that tormented King Saul always left whenever David came and worshipped with the harp (1 Samuel 16:23). In other cases, it may be appropriate to approach the Courts of Heaven. Here we make an appeal to God, our righteous and merciful Judge. And as we do, He can deal with the demonic powers without us needing to directly confront them. Though binding and loosening are still important, there are other methods of deliverance that may be safer and more effective. (More shall be spoken about the Courts of Heaven in Volume Three.)

Healing from a Distance

Jesus healed a royal official's son who was sick. The man begged Jesus to come with him for his son was dying but Jesus replied: *'You may go. Your son will live'*. Jesus chose not to go but to heal from a distance. The man believed and when he went, he found out at the same time Jesus spoke these words the fever had left his son (John 4:46-53). Likewise, a Greek Syrophoenician woman fell at Jesus' feet, begging Him to heal her daughter who was possessed by an evil spirit. Jesus responded: *'For such a reply, you may go; the demon has left your daughter'* (Mark 7:29). Due to the woman's faith, Jesus delivered her daughter of an evil spirit, without laying hands on her but praying from a distance. We too may see healings take place when we intercede or pray for others from a distance.

Rebuking the Sickness

On other occasions, Jesus simply spoke directly at the sickness and rebuked it. Simon Peter's mother-in-law was very sick with a high fever and when Jesus approached her, He rebuked the fever and it instantly left her (Luke 4:39). We too can speak directly at a sickness or disease and rebuke the symptoms in the Name of Jesus. As we take authority over the symptoms and command them to go, we then command the body or organs to be healed. This isn't necessarily commanding a demon to go, but rather commanding the body itself to be healed. It is simply taking spiritual authority over sickness, just like Jesus demonstrated. When Jesus healed the man who was deaf, He commanded the man's ears to, *'Be opened!'* (Mark 7:34).

Sometimes, for no apparent reason, I have suddenly felt a pain in a part of my body, especially when out walking. However, as soon as I have taken authority over the symptom and rebuked it, within seconds or minutes, it has gone. I believe we have authority over our bodies and can command the symptoms to go, instead of coming under them.

Jesus never became sick. I believe it was because He was without sin, but also because He walked in complete authority through unity with His Father. Every demon and sickness had to surrender to Him. None were allowed to enter Him. Since Jesus carried God's presence with power and anointing, He was essentially bringing Heaven to earth. Symptoms flee when we engage in His presence.

Raising the Dead

Jesus demonstrated with power and authority how to raise the dead. He said: *'I am the Resurrection and the Life. He who believes in Me will live, even though he dies; and whoever lives and believes in Me will never die'*. Jesus thanked His Father, then commanded Lazarus to come forth from the burial tomb: *'The dead man came out, his hands and feet wrapped with strips of linen, and a cloth around his face'* (John 11:25-43).

On another occasion, Jesus raised a widow's son from the dead. He simply commanded the young man to get up from the coffin: *'Young man, I say to you, get up!'* After Jesus touched the coffin and spoke these words, the dead man sat up and began to talk (Luke 7:14). Jesus was approached by Jairus, a synagogue ruler, when his daughter died. Jesus told Jairus: *'Don't be afraid; just believe and she will be healed'*. Jesus then went to his daughter and said: *"My child, get up!" Her spirit returned and at once she stood up'* (Matthew 9:18-24, Luke 8:49-55).

On all three occasions, Jesus commanded them to get up or come forth. As He did, their spirits returned to their bodies and life was breathed back in them. It is interesting from a medical point of view that the spirit leaves the body when someone dies, and when the spirit returned to the girl, she came back to life.

This is what the Lord spoke to Ezekiel in the Valley of Dry Bones: *'Prophesy to these bones and say to them, "Dry bones, hear the word of the Lord! This is what the Sovereign Lord says to these bones: **I will make breath enter you and you will come to life."'*** As breath entered these slain bodies, they came back to life (Ezekiel 37: 4-10). Jesus is our resurrection and our life. He said: *'The Spirit gives life; the flesh counts for nothing. The words I have spoken to you are Spirit and they are life'* (John 6:63).

Obedience and Availability

Jesus came to *do the will* of His Father (John 6:38, Matthew 7:21). He only did what He saw or heard Him doing (John 5:19, 30) and spoke only what the Father had taught Him (John 8:28). Yet, He never said no or refused anyone healing, though some had to shout louder to be heard, like the blind man who shouted: *'Jesus, Son of David, have mercy on me'* or the Gentile woman who persisted in faith, until He healed her daughter (Matthew 20:29-31, 15:21-28).

Some evenings Jesus would still be ministering: *'When evening came, many who were demon-possessed were brought to Him and He **drove out** the **spirits with a word** and healed **all the** sick'* (Mathew 4:23, 8:16). Jesus said, the words He speaks are not His own, rather it is the ***Father living in Him that is doing the work*** (John 14:10).

Jesus made Himself available to those who came across His path or to those whom His Father sent Him. He demonstrated an attitude of humility and a servant heart in all He did.

Revelation & Discernment

Jesus had revelation and discernment as to what the problem was in the person's life. He could see if the sickness was due to natural causes, or if it was due to sin or if there was a demonic spirit involved. He always took the next steps as His Father instructed, for He didn't heal those with the same sickness the same way. Revelation and discernment are required in order to know the issues or roots behind the problem and to know how to approach the case. We need to take time to hear what the Lord is whispering to our spirit, and then do as He leads.

How did the Apostles Heal the Sick?

The disciples mainly learnt by hanging out with Jesus and walking with Him. He taught them Kingdom truths and principles and showed them how to heal as He went about ministering to others. They learnt much by seeing what He did then doing it themselves, and they learnt from their mistakes because this was part of the training. Since we are all learning new things, we remain students throughout life. If we remain humble with a teachable attitude, we will keep discovering and learning new things.

Authority & Power

Jesus gave the disciples *power* and *authority* to drive out demons and cure diseases (Luke 9:1-2). They said: *'"Lord, even the demons submit to us in Your Name".* Jesus replied, *"I saw Satan fall like lightning from Heaven. I have given you **authority to trample on snakes and scorpions and to overcome all the power of the enemy; nothing will harm you"'** (Luke 10:17-20, Mark 6:7, Matthew 10:8).

The disciples had come under the same authority and power that Jesus was carrying when they worked with Him during His three years of ministry. This was a *corporate* authority and anointing that Jesus released to them as they worked alongside Him. Then came the time when they needed to receive it for themselves, in order to continue ministering under this same authority and anointing. Jesus said: *'Unless I go away, the Counselor will not come to you; but if I go, I will send Him to you.... He will guide you in all truth'* (John 16:7, 13).

When Jesus returned to His disciples after being resurrected from the dead, He said to them: *'All authority in Heaven and on earth has been given to Me'* (Mathew 28:18). If Jesus has **all** authority, then that means Satan has none. Satan has power, but no authority since he is a fallen angel and no longer in the Kingdom of God or under the authority of God. Authority in a designated area can only be given by the one whose authority in that area we are willing to submit to. If we surrender our lives to God and submit our will to Him, He will release His authority and power upon us, as He sends us His Holy Spirit to be with us. Jesus gave His disciples *authority* that would overcome *all* the *power* of the enemy.

Anointing & Commissioning

Jesus said to His disciples: *'I am going to send you what My Father has promised; but stay in the city until you have been* **clothed with power from on high**' (Luke 24:49).

The Greek word used here for power is *'dunamis'* which means dynamite or miraculous power. It was an explosive power that they were going to receive. This baptism of the Holy Spirit was going to empower the disciples for their work ahead, but they had to 'wait' for it. Jesus had already breathed on them and filled them with the Holy Spirit, on the evening of Resurrection day. The disciples were filled *again* with the Holy Spirit at Pentecost but the main thing here was that a 'violent' wind came followed by what looked like 'tongues of fire' resting on them. Also, it was 'suddenly'. Here they were receiving their 'anointing' as the Spirit came in a 'forceful' way and 'rested' on them. This was the 'clothing with power from on high' that Jesus referred to (Luke 24:49). It came in God's timing and not theirs.

God anoints us for the work that He has called us to do. It is usually received later than when we were first filled with the Holy Spirit. God chooses the timing in our life when we are ready to carry His anointing, for there is a responsibility that comes with it! Just like a father wouldn't give a young child the keys to drive a car until they were of age and maturity, so God releases His anointing on us when we are ready to carry the responsibility that comes with it. Hence, we cannot predict when an anointing will take place. It is in God's timing and He anoints everyone differently. An anointing comes by the grace of God and not by our own works.

Power in the Name of Jesus
Jesus said that we will do even greater works than Him, and He will do whatever we ask in His Name (John 14:12-14). *'I tell you the truth, My Father will give you **whatever you ask in My Name'** (John 16:23). When Jesus spoke this to the disciples, He trusted them, as His friends, to call upon His Name in a worthy manner. If what we ask is pleasing to our Father, then He will give it to us (1 John 5:14).

God gave Jesus the Name that is above all other names, that at the Name of Jesus every knee will bow in Heaven and on earth and under the earth, and every tongue confess that Jesus Christ is Lord (Philippians 2:5-11). Every living thing has to submit to the powerful Name of Jesus.

Peter came across a crippled man and said to him: *'Silver or gold I do not have but what I have I give you. **In the Name of Jesus of Nazareth, walk!'** (Acts 3:6). The man walked as he was lifted to his feet. Peter told the onlookers that the man had been healed *'by faith in the Name of Jesus'* (Acts 3:16).

Power in the Blood of Jesus
The blood of Jesus has power to cleanse, purify, heal, protect and redeem. John said that the blood of Jesus *purifies us from all sin.* And Peter stated how we have been *redeemed with the precious blood of Jesus,* and *'by His wounds (or stripes) you have been healed'* (1 John 1:5-7, 1 Peter 1:18-19, 2:24).

According to Leviticus, the life of a creature is in the blood and God had made the atonement of sin possible through the sacrifice of an animal on the altar. It is the blood that makes atonement for one's life (Leviticus 17:11). There is life in the blood and it is through the blood of Jesus that our sins can be atoned for (Hebrews 2:17).

Isaiah 53:4-5 says: *'Surely He took up our **infirmities** and carried our **sorrows,** yet we considered Him stricken by God, smitten by Him and afflicted. But He was pierced for our **transgressions,** He was crushed for our **iniquities;** the punishment that brought us peace was* upon Him and **by His wounds we are healed'.** This scripture is also referred to in Matthew 8:16-17: *'Many who were demon-possessed were brought to Him and He drove out the spirits with a word and healed all the sick. This was to fulfill what was spoken through the prophet Isaiah: "He took up our infirmities and carried our diseases"'*. Essentially what is written in Isaiah and Matthew is that the blood of Jesus not only forgives our sins but also heals us physically and emotionally, as well as delivers us from demonic spirits.

At the last supper with His disciples, Jesus took bread, broke it and gave it to His disciples saying: **'This is My body** *given for you; do this in remembrance of Me'*. After the supper He took the cup saying: *'This* **cup is the new covenant in My blood** *which is poured out for you'* (Luke 22:19-21). In Matthew's version it reads: **'This is My blood** *of the covenant, which is poured out for many for the* **forgiveness of sins'** (Matthew 26:28).

Many have experienced healing and deliverance through taking the Communion. Those who have been in any ungodly covenants can enter into a new covenant with Jesus, through accepting His blood of the 'new covenant'. Jesus said: *'This is My blood of the new covenant which is poured out for many for the forgiveness of sins,'* (Matthew 26:28, 1 Corinthians 11:25).

Many times I have felt prompted to take Communion with the Lord, whether on my own or with other believers. Each time has been a special moment. We mustn't underestimate the power in taking Communion. It is more than eating bread and drinking juice or wine. As we take it by faith, I believe it supernaturally becomes His body and blood. We must never underestimate the power in His blood, for through His blood there is healing, forgiveness of sins, cleansing of evil spirits, and protection from the evil one (Exodus 12:13).

Praying in Pairs
Jesus sent the disciples out 'two by two' when ministering to the sick (Luke 10:1, Mark 6:7). The Holy Spirit said to the church at Antioch: *'Set apart for Me Barnabas and Saul for the work to which I have called them'*. And Jesus told His disciples: *'If two of you agree about anything you ask for, it will be done for you by My Father in Heaven. For where two or three come together in My Name, there am I with them'* (Acts 13:2, Mathew 18:19).

I believe there is wisdom when praying in twos or threes. First, two are better than one when ministering and listening to God. One can be interceding, while the other is ministering. Two can also bear witness to what has taken place during the ministry and prevent any unhealthy relationships, false accusations or misinterpretations from occurring. Also, there can be greater protection and support when working alongside others compared to working alone. God enjoys it when we minister together in the power of His Spirit. Where there is unity in the Spirit amongst believers, He releases a greater measure of His anointing (Psalm 133:1-2). Hence, Jesus encouraged His disciples to pray together, in His Name, and as they did He would be with them.

Raising the Dead

Peter raised a fellow disciple, Tabitha, from the dead when asked to go to her. First he sent all the mourners out of her room, then got down on his knees and prayed. When he said: *'Tabitha, get up'*, she opened her eyes and sat up (Acts 9:40).

Paul raised a young man, Eutychus, from the dead. The man had fallen asleep and fallen from a ledge while Paul was preaching to a crowd. Paul immediately went and threw himself on the young man and he came back to life (Acts 20:7-12).

Jesus instructed His disciples to: *'Heal the sick, **raise the dead**, cleanse those with leprosy and drive out demons'* (Matthew 10:8). God has given us power and authority to raise the dead, since His Spirit gives life.

Humility & Grace

The Apostles realized they could do nothing without the power of the Holy Spirit. Jesus had already spoken this word to them before His death on the cross. He said: *'I am the vine; you are the branches. If a man remains in Me and I in him, he will bear much fruit; apart from Me you can do nothing'* (John 15:4-5). All they did came from the grace of Jesus, that is, His strength and ability to do what they couldn't do by themselves. With great power the apostles testified to the resurrection of the Lord and ***much grace*** was upon them (Acts 4:33). Stephen was a man full of God's grace and power, who performed signs and miracles among the people (Acts 6:8).

41

When Simon the sorcerer saw the Apostle's power, he wanted to have the Holy Spirit for his own selfish use. Peter discerned this and rebuked him saying: *'May your money perish with you because you thought you could buy the gift of God with money!'* (Acts 8:20).

When Jesus first sent out the twelve disciples, He told them: *'Freely you have received. Freely give'* (Matthew 10:8). All that we have received from God comes freely, whether it is salvation, the gifts of the Holy Spirit, or an anointing to minister to God's people. We have received these by His grace. We can take no credit for ourselves but freely give away that which the Holy Spirit has given us, and trust God to provide in His own way for our everyday needs.

Faith & Boldness

Peter with faith and boldness said to the crippled man: *'In the Name of Jesus, walk!'* After this, Peter and John were arrested and brought before the rulers and elders, where they were told to stop preaching in the Name of Jesus. They refused to stop, and when they were released they prayed for greater boldness to fall on them to speak God's Word. They prayed: *'Now Lord, consider their threats and enable Your servants to speak Your Word with great boldness. Stretch out Your hand to heal and perform miraculous signs and wonders through the Name of Your holy servant Jesus'*. The place where they were meeting was violently shaken, and they were filled with the Holy Spirit and spoke the Word of God **boldly** (Acts 4: 29-31). We too can ask God for holy boldness, when ministering to others.

Laying on of Hands

After Paul was shipwrecked on the island of Malta, the chief official invited him to his home. During this time, Paul noticed that the chief official's father was sick in bed. He had fever and dysentery. *'Paul went in to see him and after prayer, placed his hands on him and healed him'* (Acts 28:8).

The Lord instructed Ananias in a vision to go to Saul of Tarsus and to place his hands on him to restore his sight. So Ananias obeyed, and after placing his hands on Saul, something like scales fell from Saul's eyes and he could see again (Acts 9:11-18).

Paul encouraged Timothy to fan into the flame the gift of God which he received through the laying on of hands (2 Timothy 1:6, 1 Timothy 4:14). The laying on of hands was used to release healing and to impart the Holy Spirit to others (Acts 8:17).

Forgiveness of Sins

James said we are to confess our sins to one another, so that we may be healed: *'And the prayer offered in faith will make the sick person well; the Lord will raise him up. If he has sinned, he will be forgiven. Therefore, **confess your sins to each other and pray for each other so that you may be healed'** (James 5:15-16).

So often, sickness is due to unresolved sin. Things we have said or done may give the enemy legal access to inflict sickness or disease. We can close this open door to the enemy through repentance and forgiveness. Likewise, we must be careful not to judge others who are struggling with healing, but to see them through God's eyes. It is kindness that leads others to repentance (Romans 2:4).

Peter's Shadow

People brought the sick into the streets as Peter passed by, so that his shadow may fall and they would be healed (Acts 5:15). This has nothing to do with Peter's actual shadow but it is referring to the overflowing presence of God that Peter was carrying. When we carry His presence and anointing, power flows from us. When people are carrying the anointing, there can be an overflow of the Spirit, causing those around to be healed or slain in the Spirit, without the person touching them. It is an honour to carry His anointing. However, it requires humility and obedience to maintain such an anointing.

Paul's Handkerchief & Apron

God did extraordinary miracles through Paul, where the handkerchiefs and aprons that he touched were taken to the sick, and their illnesses were cured (Acts 19:11). This is useful when someone can't reach the person who is carrying the healing anointing. The anointing power is transferred through a piece of cloth, and this still works today.

Anointing with Oil
When Jesus sent out the disciples, they drove out many demons and **anointed many sick people with oil and healed** them (Mark 6:13). James said if anyone is sick he should get the elders of the church to pray over him and *anoint him with oil in the Name of the Lord*. And the prayer offered in *faith* will make the sick person well (James 5:13-16). Here, the anointing with oil is combined with the prayer said in faith.

We mustn't have faith in the oil but God. However, the oil refers to the oil of the Spirit (Psalm 133:2, Isaiah 61:3, Hebrews 1:9). If I am praying for someone, I may sense to anoint them with oil. I have witnessed many receive the power of the Holy Spirit in greater measure and even receive healing when I have anointed them with oil, but this has always been under the prompting of the Holy Spirit. On one occasion, I was about to anoint my team with oil, when I noticed my hands were already covered in oil. I thought the cap must have somehow come off the bottle. When I checked the bottle in my hand, the cap was still tightly sealed. I realized the Lord had poured out His supernatural oil and all who were anointed fell under the power of the Spirit.

Transported by the Spirit
Jesus and His disciples were transported by the Spirit as they were taken supernaturally from one place to another. We see that Philip was transported in the Spirit to minister to the Ethiopian eunuch (Acts 8:39). Likewise, Jesus walked straight through the crowds when they were about to throw Him off the cliff (Luke 4:30). Since this was physically impossible, then it most likely means that Jesus was transported through the crowds by the Spirit.

Today, men and women of God are being transported in the Spirit to minister healing to those who are in some form of crisis or desperate situation. God can supernaturally transport His humble men and women to other nations, to minister healing and freedom to others.

I know a humble, retired nurse, who wanted to serve God in her last years of life. She had read about people who were transported in the Spirit to minister to others who were in desperate situations.[1] So she prayed God would use her in a similar way to help others in need. Each day she prayed that the Lord would send her in the Spirit to minister to others around the world. Nothing happened for six months. Then one day, as she was praying and worshipping in His presence, she suddenly was in another country helping a person who was crying out to God. Each time, she knew exactly what to do as she ministered under the power of the Holy Spirit. Once the assignment was finished, she found herself back in her room or place of worship.

When the late American prophet, John Paul Jackson, was critically ill with pancreatitis, he cried out to God to heal him. Then, he saw an old looking, short man with white hair and wrinkly skin appear in his room. The man laid hands on his body and he was instantly healed. Then the man disappeared. The Lord revealed to him, that this was not an angel or a demon, but a humble man who asked God to use him to glorify His name. God had transported this humble man in the Spirit to minister to John Paul Jackson. The Lord can supernaturally send His servants to minister to the desperate needs of others, as we make ourselves available to serve Him in His Kingdom.

A Naturally Supernatural Lifestyle

Jesus demonstrated during His life on earth, how we can live a naturally supernatural lifestyle. He told us that we will do even greater things than Him, for He was going to the Father (John 14:12). We too can live a naturally supernatural lifestyle if we choose to live with the power of the Holy Spirit, and daily seek His council in all things. This same healing and deliverance which Jesus and His disciples did, is available for us today!

END NOTES:

[1] Bolz, Shaun; *Translating God*, Newtype, 2015
Allen, Bruce; *Gazing Into Glory*, Destiny Image, 2013

3

Holy Spirit Contract

The Spirit of the Lord is on me, because He has anointed me

Luke 4:18

God is calling us all, not just a select few, to release healing in His Kingdom. All who have the Spirit of God can heal. We simply need faith like a child. Jesus asked His Father to send us the Holy Spirit who is our Counsellor and Spirit of Truth (John 14:16). Through His Spirit working in us, we too can do the works He did. This is our Holy Spirit contract: *'To bind up the broken hearted, to proclaim freedom for the captives and release from darkness for the prisoners, to comfort all who mourn and provide for those who grieve in Zion- to bestow on them a crown of beauty instead of ashes, the oil of gladness instead of mourning, and a garment of praise instead of a spirit of despair"* (Isaiah 61:1-3).

Isaiah 61:1-3

The Spirit of the Lord is on Me, because He has Anointed Me
Jesus entered His ministry after He was anointed by the Holy Spirit to do the work God called Him to. After His resurrection, He told the disciples to wait in the city until they had been *'clothed with power from on high'* (Luke 24:49). The anointing is like a

47

mantle God gives as we carry His authority and power for the missions and service He has called us to do. When we are filled with the Spirit, the Spirit is in us and this is for ourselves. However, the anointing is when the Spirit comes upon us. This is for the ministry He has called us to, which is for the benefit of others. We must humbly receive this and guard it from any form of pride, vanity or selfish ambition. People who carry an anointing are tempted to fall into various sins. These include the abuse of power, a lust for fame or money, sexual temptations, and pride. We must guard our hearts and minds against such temptations.

To Preach Good News to the Poor
God has called us to reach the lost and spiritually poor, by revealing the Good News to those who don't know Him. This applies to us all as we meet people in our everyday lives. It's not just for the evangelists as I thought, but we are all called to be witnesses, by simply sharing with others about the love and power of Jesus.

The poor not only refers to those who lack possessions or have nothing, but also refers to those who lack the Spirit. Jesus said: *'You say, "I am rich; I have acquired wealth and do not need a thing." But you do not realize that you are wretched, pitiful, poor, blind and naked. I counsel you to buy from Me gold refined in the fire, so you can become rich; and white clothes to wear, so you can cover your shameful nakedness; and salve to put on your eyes so you can see. Those whom I love, I rebuke and discipline'* (Revelations 3:17). Many have lost their first love with Jesus and replaced it with idols such as possessions, work, relationships or even their ministry. The Holy Spirit is grieved when we do this, and wants to refine our hearts so our hearts may be back in union with Him.

I have spoken to strangers on the streets through doing something known as, *'Treasure Hunting'*[1]. Treasure hunting is hunting for Gods' treasure in His people. This is by asking the Lord for pictures and words of knowledge for the people He wants you to meet, and to write the words down on paper. He may tell you how to spot them (such as a bobble hat, blue coat, around thirty years old with a small white dog, or an old man in a wheel chair or a crippled young woman). Or He may give you a picture or name of the street where they live. When I meet people who match the description on the paper, I say something like, 'I'm looking for a treasure with this description (and show them my piece of paper) and I think it is YOU.' If this is a match and the person responds, I may give them a specific word from the Lord or ask them if they would like prayer. If the word of knowledge was for a specific ailment, such as a broken leg or blindness in one eye, then I will offer to pray for this. In my culture, I find people are encouraged when I show them what I have written, and how God has led me to minister His love and healing to them. This is the best tool I have found for healing evangelism and it is fun when done with others. (I recommend Kevin Dedmon's book: 'Treasure Hunting'[1]).

To Bind Up the Broken-Hearted

A heart attack occurs when heart muscle is starved from the blood supply of oxygen. This usually occurs when a coronary artery (that is the blood supply to the heart muscle) is blocked. When we experience emotional pain in life, unless we deal with it in a healthy way, we will end up blocking off part of our heart to God or others as part of protecting ourselves from further hurt. However, God can heal our hearts for He knows our childhood traumas and deep wounded emotions. Time simply suppresses hurts, it doesn't heal them. Otherwise, why does God want to take us back to the memories in our childhood or earlier years, to bring healing and freedom? He has not only done this for me but for countless other men and women who are now walking and living in His joy and freedom. It is one thing to be set free from demonic spirits but another thing to have our broken hearts healed by the love of God. Only God can heal our wounded hearts, through His power and unquenchable love.

At one point in life, when I experienced both betrayal and rejection by a colleague, a fellow prayer warrior saw with her spiritual eyes a spear in my back. So as she was praying, she pulled this spear out of my back and as she did, I felt immense pain within. It felt as if there was a real spear with poison on the tip. A year or so later, I thought I had dealt with this wound, until I experienced a similar situation which triggered a deep hurt within. On asking the Holy Spirit what was causing this emotional pain, He showed me that is was from the rejection I had previously felt. The truth was I had previously dealt with the spiritual aspect, but my wounded heart still needed emotionally healing with God's love. It made me think how the spirit of rejection and betrayal, are like thorns or debris in a wound. However, once the thorns or debris have been removed, the raw wound still needs healing with the soothing oil of His healing love (Hebrews 1:9). '*He heals the broken-hearted and binds up their wounds*' (Psalm 147:3).

To Proclaim Freedom for the Captives

A captive is someone who is in bondage due to another person's sin. They can be like a prisoner of war, and this may be knowingly or unknowingly. Some may have suffered some form of physical, emotional or mental abuse through what others may have said or done.

We can become captives with the thoughts that go on in our mind, especially the false beliefs or statements we have said or heard others say. These negative thoughts are from the world, flesh or devil. Paul said: '*See to it that no one takes you **captive** through **hollow and deceptive philosophy**, that depends on **human tradition** and **the basic principles of this world**, rather than on Christ*' (Colossians 2:8).

We make ourselves captives when we follow human tradition and culture, or believe the lies from the enemy, instead of accepting the truth from Jesus. Many people are not aware of living in captivity through the lies or fears they believe. The Holy Spirit needs to bring revelation to the truth to free our minds from such captive thoughts.

To free captives is to free people from the negative experiences that others may have inflicted. This includes freeing from curses, witchcraft, false guilt, false blame, shame, lies, false beliefs, fears, control, betrayal, rejection and abandonment. This includes setting people free from the deception and lies they have believed, and replacing it with the truth of how the Father sees them.

Paul said: '*For though we live in the world, we do not wage war as the world does. The weapons we fight with are not the weapons of the world. On the contrary, they have **divine power** to **demolish*** *strongholds. We demolish arguments and every pretension that sets itself up against the knowledge of God and we take captive every thought to make it obedient to Christ'* (2 Corinthians 10:3-5).

We can choose not to live under false beliefs, accusations or lies about who we are (or what others say), but instead ask God for His truth. God will always reveal His truth if we ask Him how He really sees us or the truth for a given situation. We hear many things that are not from God and need to filter these thoughts from our minds. We may struggle to hear God when we don't take captive our thoughts. Prayerfully, we take captive our thoughts and surrender them to God, commanding anything not from Him to leave. We can ask Him for His truth and direction in all things. Paul said: *'Be transformed by the renewing of your mind'* (Romans 12:2). It is a daily choice to renew our minds as we seek God and His truth in all things.

When I was seeking the Lord for healing over a particular issue in my life, I was surprised when He took me back to a time in my childhood. He brought to memory the time I was alone in a cot on a hospital ward. I was around one year of age and had measles. Though I had no conscious recall of this incident, the Holy Spirit revealed this memory through my spirit. In the memory, I felt abandoned and developed the fear of being alone. Then I saw a spiritual dark presence coming over my cot, and myself standing in the cot crying. On realising this, I (now as an adult) prayed and took authority over the spirits of abandonment, rejection, fear and loneliness and commanded them to leave in the Name of Jesus. Then I asked Jesus where He was in this situation. Immediately, I saw Him come and pick me up with the light of His presence surrounding me. Then I realized I wasn't abandoned, but it was a lie from the enemy. It was actually a 'perceived' sense of rejection and abandonment. When I saw myself playing with Jesus in my cot with His Presence surrounding me, I rebuked the lie that had fed into my mind, and accepted the truth that Jesus will never leave or abandon me, even when I feel alone. Jesus loves to set us free with His Spirit and truth, when we invite Him into our hearts.

On another occasion, I had believed a lie that my relationship with God was about achievement. The Lord showed me I didn't have to achieve anything to be His child, but to simply have fun and enjoy being with Him. My mind was set free from this captive thought when I realized this truth.

To Release the Prisoners from Darkness

A prisoner is someone who has been imprisoned as a result of the sin or crime they have committed. That means they are guilty for what they have done and would normally deserve punishment. It is only through God's mercy and love that we are forgiven and released from the punishment our sins deserve.

Jesus has paid the price for our sins. Though He has paid the price, we still need to repent and seek His forgiveness for each sin. It is like Jesus coming to our prison cell with the key for the lock and saying, 'I have forgiven you and paid your debt. Come out'. Then we follow Him from the darkness that imprisons us into His amazing light and experience a true freedom within. We can each experience this when we truly repent of all our sins and choose to turn to Him.

Also, we are imprisoned when we choose not to forgive. Unforgiveness will keep us in bondage. Jesus referred to this in the parable of the unforgiving servant. A man was in debt and owed his master much money. He begged his master to have mercy and not punish him for failing to pay back what he owed. The master went a step further and cancelled his debt, and then let him go. Another servant owed this same man some money. The servant begged for mercy but the man chose not to forgive him, but instead threw him into prison until he paid back his debt. When the master heard what this man had done to his fellow servant, he punished the man and threw him in prison. Jesus said this is how God will treat us if we refuse to forgive others from our heart (Mathew 18:21-35).

God's forgiveness cancels our debt. Debt is referring to what we owe as a result of the sins committed. If we are willing to forgive others and let them off the hook, then God will forgive us and let us off the hook for our sins. Forgiveness is a key that unlocks our prison doors and sets us free.

When God called me to a war-torn nation in Africa, one of the things I ended up doing each week was visiting the local prison and reaching out to the prisoners with God's love and healing power. I saw how the majority of the male prisoners had little, if any, experience of a father's love. Either their natural fathers had died, were never there, or they had beaten them and were incapable of showing any love to them. When I asked if they wanted to know the Heavenly Father's love, nearly all their hands went up and tears were in their eyes. They repented of their sins and crimes that had caused them to be in prison. They forgave their fathers for not being there, or for beating them. Then we asked God to reveal His Father's love in a powerful and real way. The pastors who were with me were able to embrace the men, so they could experience the power of God's love in a tangible way. There was weeping as the prisoners were like boys who were desperately reaching out for their Father's love and acceptance.

It was a powerful time and a privilege to see God minister His Father's love to each man who was open to forgive and receive forgiveness. They were experiencing an inner freedom and love like never before. I then realised how the real prisoners were not those inside the prison walls, but those still in spiritual bondage wandering outside the walls.

Some men were released much sooner than their sentence. The authorities were able to see they had changed and were no longer a threat to society. Some of them left to become pastors in their home village for they wanted others back home to experience and know God in a real way as they did. One prisoner was the son of a pastor, but had chosen the path of adultery and alcohol, and through a car accident ended up in prison. It was in prison that he came back to his senses, just like the prodigal son. He repented and wanted to get right with God. His father was praying that God would minister to him and transform his life while he was in prison. He too was released sooner than his sentence and went back to join his father in ministry. God wants to set the prisoners free but it has to start first with our own hearts.

Recovery of Sight for the Blind

God wants to open our eyes to see Him, and to see things from His heavenly perspective. Deception, false beliefs and negative experiences stop us from seeing through clear spiritual lenses. We need to ask the Lord what has tinted or brought dirt to our lenses and stopped us seeing Him? As we repent, we can ask Him to open our eyes to see Him and all He wants to reveal.

Elisha prayed: *'"O Lord, open his eyes so he may see." Then the Lord opened the servant's eyes and he looked and saw the hills full of horses and chariots of fire all around Elisha'* (2 Kings 6:17). God can heal and sharpen our natural sight but more importantly, we need our spiritual sight sharpened. Our five natural senses are also spiritual senses, so we can see, hear, smell, taste and feel in the Spirit. We can choose to see things as they are through our natural lenses, or ask God to show us what is really taking place through our supernatural lenses. This is how we learn to see things through His perspective, for His ways and thoughts are different to ours (Isaiah 55:8).

To Comfort All who Mourn, Pouring on His Oil of Gladness

To know His comfort is to experience His presence during difficult circumstances in life. The word comfort comes from *'comforte'* and this means 'with strength'. Though mourning is a natural part of life, for some it becomes like a toxin that prevents them moving on. I have seen faces change from displaying grief and despair, to becoming radiant, as they received His Spirit of hope and gladness. People feel they can start to live again once they are released from the spirit of grief or death.

I experienced His comfort during the time my sister died of a genetic illness called cystic fibrosis. His comfort felt like a huge, warm soft blanket surrounding me, and it gave me an inner strength to continue with life, knowing I would meet her one day in Heaven.

There was an African lady who wanted some medication for her neck pain. Her neck pain started after the loss of two of her children who died in a car accident caused by a drunk driver. After such shock and grief she had been living in a daze, and not been able to think straight for herself or her other children. However, she agreed to forgive the drunk driver and asked Jesus to heal her heart. Not only did her neck pain go, she commented she could start living her life again. She had been healed and freed from her pain and mourning, and in return received His comfort and the oil of His gladness. She left the clinic with a smile on her face.

An elderly man had felt life wasn't worth living after his wife died. He too felt like he had undergone a death. After praying for him and breaking off the spirit of death and grief, he was able to see life through new lenses and felt an inner strength and joy to start his life afresh, no longer on his own, but now with a new companion- the Holy Spirit.

I met an elderly man in Zimbabwe who asked me to pray for him. He had numbness down both sides of his body and had suffered ill health since one of his sons committed suicide three years ago. I sensed he was carrying grief, shame and guilt. As he gave his son to God, along with his grief, shame and guilt, the Lord started to heal him. Tears rolled down his cheek as he felt God's healing presence. His numbness instantly disappeared as life returned to his soul and spirit.

To Give a Crown of Beauty Instead of Ashes
Ashes were marked on a person's forehead during a time of mourning or deep repentance. This was accompanied by the tearing of clothes or wearing of sackcloth. Tamar put ashes on her head and tore her robes after she had been raped by her half-brother (2 Samuel 13:19). When Mordecai heard of the order sent out by Haman to destroy all the Jews, he tore his clothes, put on sackcloth and ashes and went out wailing loudly and bitterly (Ester 4:1). Jesus speaks of God's people repenting with sackcloth and ashes (Mathew 11:21).

It says in Psalms: *'You turned my wailing into dancing; You removed my sackcloth and clothed me with joy'* (Psalm 30:11). God wants to restore back to us the inner beauty and joy we lose through either sin, abuse or some death in our lives. He takes away the lifeless ashes and replaces them with His crown of beauty.

What the enemy has destroyed in our lives, God can take and somehow resurrect or bring good out of it. He is able to give back life and beauty, or restore the years the locusts have eaten. As we hand the things in our life over to Jesus, we lay them at the cross so He can resurrect them with His supernatural power.

To Put on a Garment of Praise Instead of a Spirit of Despair

People may carry a spirit of despair, oppression or depression where they feel hopeless, suicidal or there is no way out. Depression is a cloud of negative beliefs and negative emotions that weigh us down. As we give Jesus each negative thought and feeling, He will exchange them for the truth of His Spirit. His truth not only heals, but sets us free. Instead of being under the spirit of despair we can encounter His freedom and joy. It is like exchanging a cloak of despair with a cloak of joy and praise. I have seen people under the oppression of the enemy, but after prayer, burst forth into spontaneous praise and worship. It was as if a light turned on inside them.

One lady from an African village poured out her emotional distress to me as she shared about the many deaths that had taken place in her family. She was very distressed and had suffered much grief. The Spirit of God came upon me as I prayed for her and declared His oil of gladness upon her. She then started praising God and looked upwards with her arms raised high in the air. Her face now shone with such radiance you wouldn't have thought it was the same person. She was a testimony to the oil of His gladness replacing her mourning, and having a garment of praise instead of a spirit of despair. It was so beautiful to see.

Labourers for His Harvest

God is looking for sons and daughters who will come and co-labour with Him in His harvest fields. One day the Lord showed me His harvest fields in a vision. In each harvest field there were children of varying ages. The young ones were given sickles to harvest the crops while the older sons (and daughters) had been given the responsibility of driving the heavy machinery. Our Heavenly Father loaned various tools to His children, giving them the appropriate tools depending on their level of growth and maturity. He gave advanced tools to those who were more mature in their faith and character. The beautiful thing was that the children didn't boast about their allotted fields or their tools or what they had done. Instead, they found it a privilege and honour to work alongside their Father. They delighted in serving Him, knowing the tools were His and each had been assigned a field depending on their level of spiritual growth and maturity. It was recognised as 'family business'.

We all have to start somewhere in the healing ministry. The more we step out, the more we experience. And the more we experience, then the more we have to give away.

END NOTES

[1] Dedmon, Kevin; *The Ultimate Treasure Hunt,* (Destiny Image, 2007).

4

Hearing God

When He, the Spirit of Truth comes, He will guide you into all truth.

John 16:13

Listening to God is an essential part of spiritual healing and sonship. Jesus said: '*It has been written by the prophets*, "*They will all be taught by God Himself*"' (John 6:46 referring to Isaiah 54:13, Jeremiah 31:34). John said we can approach God with confidence when we pray or ask Him for anything according to His will, because when we do, *He hears us* (1 John 5:14-15). An important part of walking in freedom is to hear His truth. This comes as we learn to listen to His voice and discern His Spirit. His sheep hear His voice simply because they have learnt how to engage with His Spirit.

A key to hearing is having a hunger to be with Him. God desires to speak to our heart and spirit. This may be either from His Spirit to our spirit, from His heart to our heart or through 'impressions' of the mind. We make it seem hard, when in actuality it is easier than we think. We simply need to learn how to position our heart and spirit to hear Him.

Most of us hear God through our senses, especially our hearing, seeing and feeling. We hear an audible (external) or non-audible (internal) voice, or hear God through the voices of others.

Likewise, we may see in the Spirit with pictures, visions, dreams and impressions. Some feel and sense God's presence, as God speaks through their senses. Some may have a word of knowledge concerning an area of the body God wants to heal. Others may feel pain or discomfort in an area of their body as a sign of God wanting to heal this problem in another person's body.

God desires to speak to you and me every moment of the day. The problem is we are the ones who don't give Him the opportunity. Either we allow ourselves to get easily distracted, or don't believe He wants to speak to us, or live under the lie that we can't hear Him. However, the truth is we have all heard Him speak though we may not have been aware, simply because we didn't recognise this was His Spirit.

Laying Down a Fleece

One of the simple ways to hear is to lay down a 'fleece'. When Gideon wanted to know if he had heard from God, he put down a fleece and asked for a sign: *'If now I have found favour in Your eyes, give me a **sign that it is really You talking to me**'*. He continued, *'If You will save Israel by my hand as You have promised- look, I will place a wool fleece on the fleshing floor. If there is dew only on the fleece and all the ground is dry, then I will know that You will save Israel by my hand as You have said'* (Judges 6:17+37). God did as Gideon asked and confirmed He was with him. However, Gideon didn't just rely on a single answer, but laid another fleece down. He asked God a second time to confirm if he really heard Him. The second time, he asked God to do the opposite; this time to make the fleece dry and the ground covered with dew. When God did as Gideon asked, he knew this was no coincidence, but clearly and unmistakably it was a yes from God.

Sometimes, I have 'laid down a fleece' to ask God to show me if something is or isn't His will. However, it is good to lay down more than one fleece, like Gideon, so we can rule out any coincidences. Equally, we can ask God to confirm through other ways.

In the Old Testament it was the prophets and priests who heard God, but in the New Testament, Jesus came to make it possible for us all to hear His voice. Normally, only a high priest could enter the Most Holy Place and he did this once a year on the Day of Atonement, or *Yom Kippur*. This was the day when the priest asked God for the forgiveness of his sins and the sins of the people. However, Jesus became our Great High Priest, and stood in the gap between man and God by taking on our sins Himself. Hence, it was through His sacrificial death on the cross that He made a way for us to have access to the Heavenly Father. Since Jesus is our Great High Priest, we can come directly to Him for the forgiveness of sins.

God desires for us to build up the Body of Christ through preaching, prayer, prophecy and teaching. However, unless we take time to seek God for ourselves, we will not grow in our relationship with Him. Growth comes from personal time set aside to hear Him. We can't rely solely on what others say, but need to know for ourselves when God is speaking, as with Gideon and the fleece.

How to Hear His Voice

There are three simple steps to help us hear God and to be fed by Him. This can be highlighted in the feeding of the five thousand (Matthew 14:13). First, Jesus fed the people because they were *hungry* for His bread. He is the Bread of Life, because His living and revelatory Word is our spiritual bread and fresh manna from Heaven (John 6:10 +35). The second thing was He made them sit down and *rest*. They were not to strive or toil but to simply rest. Finally, they *fixed their eyes and heart* on Him. And as they did, they waited on the Lord. They expectantly believed He would feed them.

Hunger For God
One of the most important things to help us hear God is a hunger to be with Him. Most of us rush off to work or always have things to do, instead of taking time to be with God. If a relationship matters then we will make time to be with the person. Jesus regularly spent time alone with His Father, listening to Him, being with Him and seeking His will. He got up early each

morning or spent the night hours alone with Him. His relationship with His Father was the most important thing. Hence, He always made time to be with Him. *'Very early in the morning while it was still dark, Jesus got up, left the house and went off to a solitary place where He prayed'* (Mark 1:35). *'Each evening He went out to spend the night on the hill called the Mount of Olives'* (Luke 21:37). He said: *'For I have come down from heaven not to do My will but to do the will of Him who sent Me,'* (John 6:38). The more we seek Him and hang out with Him, the more our ears will become finer tuned to hearing Him.

Enter His Rest

As we spend more time with God, we will discover how to enter His rest. We enter His rest through humility and with a surrendered heart. As we begin to experience His awesome presence, our hunger will increase. Sometimes He may be right with us, though we cannot feel His presence. He is simply seeing how much we love Him and are willing to pursue Him. Once we discover how to commune with His Spirit, we will be able to be with Him any part of the day. The Lord desires a 24:7 relationship. This is where we commune with Him throughout the day and are aware of His presence even at night. A man known as Brother Lawrence discovered how to daily commune with God. As he communed with God doing his daily chores, he became aware of His presence. His letters describe how to *Practice the Presence of God.*[1]

People may ask, 'Why can others hear God or see things in the Spirit and I can't?' It may be because there are some spiritual or emotional blockages. However, if we want to hear Him, we simply need to put time aside to seek His presence.

Fix Our Eyes and Heart on Him

One of the reasons we may struggle to hear God is because we don't believe He wants to speak to us, or we believe the lie that we are not important. Some of us believe this because our parents didn't listen to us or were unable to provide the quality time we needed. If God can speak through a donkey, as He did to Balaam, then He can find ways to speak to each one of us (Numbers 22:28). We need to forgive our parents for not listening to us, or for speaking harsh words. As we forgive them, we can ask God to speak from His heart to ours. His words will be special and just for YOU! This comes as we learn to fix our eyes and heart on Him, and this may involve waiting on Him.

One of the first things God ever said to me was, *'Be still and know that I am God'* (Psalm 46:10). As these words entered my mind, I experienced His presence. I happened to be 'waiting' for a bus when this occurred. Waiting on God is a lost art. It is to be pro-active, like waiting for a bus, because we are expecting Him to turn up. The prophet Isaiah knew how to wait on the Lord: *'Those who wait on the Lord will renew their strength,'* (Isaiah 40:31). The Hebrew word used here for 'wait' is *'Qavah'* [2] and means to wait expectantly with our mind focused on God. Some may posture their bodies as they wait on Him. They may kneel, lie down or sit in a humble position with their legs uncrossed. There is no right way, but simply find a posture with your body yielded, and your heart and mind open to Him. There is no rush, but rather a slowing down so we may focus our hearts and minds on Him. Some may prefer to be away from their home due to noise or distractions. Others may find a secret place to be alone with Him. God loves walking with us, resting with us, playing with us and simply 'being' with us. Whatever works best for you, do it.

Some of us may get impatient and keep looking at the clock, instead of giving our time to Him. As we wait for Him, He will come. The more we are prepared to wait, the greater we will experience His presence and the deeper we will connect with Him.

One of the ways we connect to God is through worship, especially by giving Him thanks and praise. When we pray in our spiritual language (the gift of tongues), our spirit becomes connected to His Spirit and this helps us focus on Him. If you don't have this gift, you can ask for it. It is freely given by the Holy Spirit to all Spirit-filled believers. Ask and don't give up asking, and He will give it to you. Seek Him and don't give up seeking, and you will find Him (Matthew 7:7, TPT).

The Different Ways God Speaks

Peter quoted from the book of Joel: *'In the last days God says, "I will pour out My Spirit on all people. Your sons and daughters will prophesy, your young men will see visions, your old men will dream dreams"'* (Acts 2:17). Visions, dreams and prophecies, are to be the norm for everyone!

Sometimes God has to do outrageous things simply to get our attention. He chose to speak to Balaam through the mouth of a donkey because that was the only way He could get him to listen (Numbers 22:28). We need to be open to the different ways God can speak, for He may speak however He chooses. Let's look at some of these ways.

Written Word of God

The most common way we hear God speak is through the Bible. However, we need to be careful we don't just select words we like and discard those we don't, but instead invite the Holy Spirit to open our minds and hearts to His living Word. There are many hidden mysteries in the scriptures, waiting to be unravelled through the revelation of His Spirit, and through looking at the original Hebrew, Greek or Aramaic translations.

In order for the written Word to minister to our spirit, we first need to know the Author who wrote the Bible. His Word comes alive and active as we read or hear it. It gives life, for Jesus is the Author of life (Acts 3:15). We must be careful when we hear the word of God spoken by others, for it may be misinterpreted to suit what the person wants to say. If the spoken word is from the Spirit of God, then our spirits will come alive. However, if the spoken word is from the flesh, then it will minister to our flesh. If it is from a source which is not of God, then it will carry ungodly fruit such as gossip, anger, pride, fear, control, lies, heresy or condemnation.

When Jesus spoke to the disciples on the road to Emmaus, their hearts were burning when He opened up the scriptures (Luke 24:32). This is what it should be like when the Holy Spirit gives us fresh revelation of the Word of God. It should make our spirit come alive, and feel as if we are hearing or reading it for the first time. The Spirit-breathed Word of God is alive and active, sharper than any two edged sword (Hebrews 4:12).

We can go deeper when reading the Word of God by choosing to *meditate* on it. This is like chewing it over and digesting it well, so all the goodness is taken from it. Through this process, we invite God to speak at the different levels in the passage. This is where our sanctified imagination helps. We can imagine the scene as if it was happening and ask these questions: *What do I see Jesus doing? Where do I see myself in it? What do I see taking place? What do I feel, smell and hear? What is Jesus saying to me now?* Meditating on the Word of God requires time and is not to be rushed, but instead entered into under the guidance of the Holy Spirit. We can simply invite Him to speak to us by surrendering our mind (including imagination), will and emotions to Him.

The Word of God is for spiritual growth, to reveal God's character and His ways. It is also the sword of the Spirit. Hence, it is a weapon we use to fight and overcome the works of the enemy (Ephesians 6:17). Jesus replied to Satan as He was tempted in the desert, *'It is written…'* (Luke 4: 4+8+12). He quoted the scriptures to quench the fiery darts of the enemy.

Spoken Word of God (Rhema)
God speaks through His written Word but also directly through His Holy Spirit. This may be Holy Spirit breathed words of scripture or Holy Spirit breathed words directly from the mouth of God. When we use this to build up one another it is the gift of prophecy. Prophecy simply means knowing what is on God's heart at that moment in time whether for ourselves or someone else. It is the Holy Spirit speaking to our spirit or through our spirit to others. This is for everyone and not just a select few.

We can receive the spoken word of God through the gifts of the Spirit, such as the word of knowledge, word of wisdom, discernment, tongues and interpretation of tongues, as well as prophecy (1 Corinthians 12:7-11). The testimony of Jesus is the Spirit of prophecy (Revelation 19:10). Jesus bears witness to us through His Spirit.

There are many false prophets in the world and the Bible warns us of them. False prophets speak to your flesh and tell you what you want to hear. They do not point the way to Jesus. We mustn't confuse someone who is a false prophet with someone who is simply learning how to hear God and making errors in the process. Many who love the Lord may sometimes give inaccurate words to others. It is part of their training and maturing in sonship, as they are developing their ability to hear God. As we learn to listen to God, we will make mistakes. Hence, we need to discern what we hear and check it out with God. A true prophet will carry the Holy Spirit, and speak to your spirit and point you to God. When the Holy Spirit rested on the Apostles on the day of Pentecost, they spoke the word of God through fresh anointing and revelation of the Spirit.

Journaling

Writing is a helpful tool for hearing God, as we engage our hearts with His Spirit. It is for everyone who is hungry to hear God. Some call it 'prophetic writing'.

We can engage with God's Spirit simply by surrendering our body, soul and spirit to Him. As we yield to His Spirit and focus on Him, we are tuning our spirits to hear Him. Likewise, it is good to cleanse our heart, mind, imagination and spirit through the sanctifying power of His blood. As we focus our hearts on Him, we can invite the Holy Spirit to speak to our spirit. Some may have specific words, scriptures or pictures. If so, we can write them down. Or simply write down the words as they flow. I may start with a phrase like, 'My precious daughter' or 'My love.' Use whatever feels right for you. To do this properly, we mustn't try to analyze or work out what we are writing, but write it down as it flows through our spirit. We can then review what we have written after the words stop flowing. This is not to be confused with writing our thoughts down after having reflected on them first- that is different. Here, we are letting the Holy Spirit speak to our spirit, and writing down the words as they flow, then reflecting on them afterwards. The words bypass our mind (that is, we don't process them first) because it is Spirit to spirit. This is why it is a good tool to use when our mind is all over the place trying to work things out and struggling to hear God. It is easy to do when we have surrendered our all to God and invite Him to speak. To do this requires faith, where we believe He will speak to us.

You have complete control of the writing and can stop at any time. It is not 'automatic writing' which is the counterfeit version by which a demon controls the writing. Here the person has no control. Journaling feels natural, as if someone is speaking thoughts to your mind as you write them down. God will usually speak to us through our own language. Hence, the style we write sounds similar to the way we speak.

If we are seeking an answer to a question, then it is wise to use another method in addition to this for confirmation. This is to avoid writing down what we want God to say and missing what the Holy Spirit is really telling us. We must make sure that there is no personal bias when using this tool but a complete openness of our heart to whatever God wants to say. This means we need to lay down all our opinions and personal desires beforehand. This is to prevent our flesh getting in the way.

Some find it easier to write a love letter to God first. This is when we write down what is on our heart to God, then by faith write down a love letter from God to ourselves as we ask His Spirit to speak to our spirit. If this is done on a regular basis, the written words can be read again at a later date and a theme or bigger picture will be seen to emerge in what God has been speaking. We can do this to encourage ourselves in the Lord, or ask the Lord to give us a word of encouragement for someone else.

Usually, I wait on God to give me a picture or word and then I write down the words His Spirit speaks to my spirit. I find they all connect together, even with references to scripture. Usually a scripture comes to mind to confirm the words I have written. However, if what we write is against what is written in the scriptures, then we should discard it and not accept it as being from God because He doesn't go against His Word. His Word is to confirm what we are hearing is from Him. I have found this to be a valuable way to hear God, especially during difficult seasons, because I've discovered He can always speak to my spirit. This method bypasses our logic, fears, control, common sense and reasoning that gets in the way and prevents us from hearing Him.

In summary, I have found this to be valuable:

♥ *Surrender our body, soul and spirit to God so we come under the influence of His Spirit.*

♥ *Command anything of the world, flesh or devil including distractions, to go in Jesus' Name.*

♥ *Lay down all opinions or desires, so our heart is fully open to hear what the Lord wants to say to us.*

♥ *Cleanse and sanctify our heart, mind and imagination with the blood of Jesus.*

♥ *Ask for the Lord to speak to our spirit, through pictures, or words, and believe He is going to, by faith.*

♥ *Then write down the words as they come to our mind. More words will flow as we start to write. Then we can read after the flow of words stops, otherwise the analytical part of our mind will interfere with the flow of the Spirit.*

Some may ask, 'How do I know the words are from God and not just my own words?' The answer is it will bear witness to His character and nature, and the words you write will not seem like yours. They will be tender, loving or convicting but focused on God's heart and ways. They will sound like they are from His heart. Also, they will touch or minister to your heart as you read them. On the other hand, words from the enemy will bring condemnation and accusation. Some may find this easier to do than others. Initially, it is good to test what we have written by giving it to someone else who hears the Lord. This will encourage us to hear Him more.

Dreams & Visions

Dreams and visions are another way God loves to communicate to His people. A vision is a picture in motion similar to watching a clip of a film. We can have day visions or night visions. Visions may occur in dreams, where we encounter God in our sleep. During the night, God spoke to King Solomon, and asked him what he wanted? Solomon asked for wisdom and discernment, and God gave it him (1 Kings 3:5-8, 2 Chronicles 1:7).

Visions may be open or closed. In open visions you see with your eyes open, like a TV screen playing in front of you. During closed visions you see with your eyes shut. Paul had a vision of a man from Macedonia calling him to come. This was a straightforward vision with no interpretation required (Acts 16:9-10). However, Peter's vision required interpretation (Acts 10:9-18). The Bible actually describes Peter's vision as a trance. A trance is an interactive vision, where you are in the vision and not just observing it from the outside. Usually, you are not aware of your surroundings when caught up in a trance until it finishes.

Some dreams and visions may be straightforward and need no interpretation, but most need interpretation. Visions are easier to understand and remember than dreams. Since dreams have symbolic meanings, we have to learn what things represent or symbolize, and this is where we can ask the Holy Spirit to give us further understanding and revelation. It is good to write down our dreams and visions because the revelation or understanding may come later as things unfold in life.

Night terrors are demonic dreams. They may include flashbacks of traumatic memories. For example, a child had recurrent night terrors after watching a film. After taking authority over the fear, the night terrors ceased.

Dreams may carry warnings, or may release healing, prophecy or training. It is good to write down dreams as soon as we awake, and while they are fresh. If they come with a warning then we can respond through prayer or with the appropriate action needed.

Pictures

A picture is a visual snapshot of something. Pictures may be simple and straightforward, while others require interpretation. A friend once had a picture of me dressed as a nurse, holding a book with a red cross on it. This was when I was a hospital doctor so it made no sense. My friend then had this revelation from the Holy Spirit: Jesus was the Doctor and I was His nurse. He would lead me to those He wanted me to help, then tell me their diagnosis and how to treat them. My book wasn't a medical book but the Bible. This carried a different meaning about a call to serve God in His Kingdom (you can read more about this in my book, *'Healing God's Way'*).

Sometimes we may have a picture for someone else, and it means nothing to us but everything to the person whom it is given. God knows how to speak to us! We must not be discouraged to share the pictures we have received, if they appear strange or meaningless. The chance is they will mean everything to the person whom they are for. This shows God knows how to speak to us individually and intimately. If He gives us a picture for someone, we can humbly say, 'I have this picture and don't know if it means anything to you...' If it means nothing, then the person can discard it. However, it is most likely that it will mean something! Likewise, for those who are more prophetic, we can ask God what does the picture mean or what does it refer to in the person's life. This is known as receiving a revelation followed by an interpretation.

Revelations

The Greek word for revelation is *apokalypsis,* which means to reveal what is hidden or to make information known so it can be understood. A revelation is when you have a thought that you know isn't of your own thinking, but is from God. It is like a light being turned on with sudden understanding and insight into a situation. It can be compared to seeing in a way that you couldn't see before, or when something new is suddenly revealed that you didn't know before. You know this insight or revelation is from the Holy Spirit. Jesus tells His disciples that He will send us the Holy Spirit who will be our Counsellor and will teach us all things (John 14:26). This teaching and understanding is through revelation from the Holy Spirit. The Jews were amazed at what they heard Jesus teach and asked: *"How did this man get such learning without having studied?" Jesus answered, "My teaching is not My own. It comes from Him who sent Me"* (John 7:15-16). Jesus' teachings came from fresh revelations from the Father.

Jesus said that Peter's revelation of Him being the Son of God, was given to Him by His Father and not by man (Matthew 16:17). Sometimes, I may have a flash thought when God wants to speak to me about something. A thought may suddenly come to mind which I know is not my own thinking, especially when my mind is on something else. God desires us to seek Him so He can reveal more mysteries and truths through the revelation of His Spirit. When others share a Holy Spirit revelation, it will immediately minister to our spirit. God reveals truth from His Spirit to our spirit.

Riddles & Proverbs

God can also speak to us through riddles and modern day proverbs. One day I asked the Lord for the name of the ministry He wanted me to pioneer. To my surprise I had the word 'THEO'. I knew Theo was from the Greek word *Theos*, meaning God. So, I asked Him how this word could explain the type of ministry He was calling me to. Next, I realized THEO was an anagram and each letter stood for something. Immediately I had: T- Transforming lives, H- Healing hearts, E- Equipping and empowering the body of Christ, O- Overcoming the enemy. This perfectly described the ministry. In the book of Proverbs we read it is the glory of God to conceal a matter but the glory of kings to search it out (Proverbs 25:2).

During another time, when I had a fear of going to the dark nations (or places where there is little or no light of Jesus shining in the lives of the people), God gave me a modern day proverb. He said something like this, *'It is safer to be with Me in a dangerous place than it is to be on your own in a safe place'*. This gave me immediate peace for following Him into dark nations. I had nothing to fear for He was with me and that was what mattered. The safest place to be is in the will of God, for when we are in His will, we are in His presence.

Jesus constantly spoke to the people and His disciples in parables and through figurative speech. This was to conceal it from the worldly wise, including the Pharisees, but to reveal it to God's children through His Spirit. Paul said: *'The man without the Spirit does not accept the things that come from the Spirit of God, for they are foolishness to him **and he cannot understand them, because they are spiritually discerned'*** (1Corinthians 2:14).

Speaking Through Our Senses

We have five natural and five spiritual senses. God can speak to us through our feelings, taste, smell, hearing and sight. He can speak to us through these senses with the gift of discernment. The

Bible says that our *senses are trained to distinguish between good and evil* (Hebrews 5:14, NASB). Some say we have two eyes and two ears so we can hear and see spiritually through one and naturally through the other. We are not to judge others by what we see with our eyes or hear with our ears but with what we see and hear the Holy Spirit is saying for each given situation (Isaiah 11:3).

Smell

Usually when we smell things in the Spirit, it is either pleasant or foul. Sweet smells, like the aroma of flowers, represents His presence and goodness. However, foul smells, like sulphurous bad eggs, are usually indicative of demonic spirits. Sometimes people give off a bad odour when they are delivered from a demonic spirit. Once I smelt a foul smell coming from someone standing behind me during a time of worship. It was so foul it was distracting me from worship, so I quietly took authority over it in Jesus' Name and commanded it to go. Within seconds it disappeared and could be smelt no more. Paul said: *'Thanks be to God who always leads us in triumphal procession in Christ and through us spreads everywhere the fragrance of the knowledge of Him. For we are to God the aroma of Christ,'* (2 Corinthians 2:14).

Feelings and Touch

Feelings from God include His love, peace, joy or a stirring in our spirit when His Spirit is drawing our attention to something. Likewise, we may experience unpleasant feelings that represent warnings from God or indicate we are not in His will. This may be when we sense an unease, confusion, or restlessness in our spirit. Likewise, we may feel a warmth or peace when we are in God's presence, but a cold shiver when encountering a demonic presence. People may experience pain in their bodies when God is giving them words of knowledge for someone else with similar pain He wants to heal. There are many things we can sense or feel that are or aren't of God. We may sense oppression when we come up against demonic spirits others may be carrying. The opposite is true when we are in God's presence or meet others who are filled with the Holy Spirit. We learn to discern our feelings and senses; what is of His Spirit and what is from the enemy.

God may speak when we *touch* someone. Many times a word or spiritual insight has come to my mind when I have touched a person. On some occasions, my hand may feel hot as I sense God's healing power. Once, when I put my hand on a friend and prayed for her, she commented afterward that she felt the hand of God where my hand was. God can minister powerfully to us through a touch or a hug, as if it is His hand touching or Himself hugging.

One of the ways we can powerfully reveal God's Father-heart to those who have never experienced His love is through an embrace. Some experience God's love for the first time through a father's embrace. We simply need to be sensitive to the prompting of the Spirit when to do this.

Sight

God can open our eyes to see in the supernatural if we ask Him. Elisha prayed that his servant would see in the supernatural realm as they were being attacked by enemies. He prayed: '*Oh Lord, open his eyes so he may see*' (2 Kings 6:17). After this his servant saw God's horses and chariots of fire all over the hills outnumbering their enemies.

When Jesus healed the man born blind, He not only restored his natural sight but the man's spiritual eyes were opened, as he realised Jesus was the Son of God (John 9:35-39). We can ask the Lord to increase our ability to see things in the Spirit and from His perspective.

The Lord has given us an imagination. The enemy has tried to pollute and defile it with obscene and fearful thoughts. However, we can cleanse and sanctify our imagination through the power of His blood and by surrendering it to Him. Then by faith, we can engage our spirit with His Spirit, and start to see things (through our sanctified imagination) in the spiritual and heavenly realms.

Hearing

God may speak to some with an audible voice. This is an externally heard voice, as if another person is speaking to us. Samuel heard God speak this way (1 Samuel 3:10). Paul heard Jesus speak audibly on the road to Damascus. To those around it sounded like thunder (Acts 9: 3-7). For most of us, we hear God speak through a non-audible or internal voice. His Spirit speaks to our spirit, and thoughts enter our mind as we converse with Him. I believe many people, especially non-Christians, who 'hear voices' speaking to them may be hearing demonic spirits, and definitely when the voice tells them to commit suicide or do evil things. Hence, we need to discern if what we are hearing is from the Holy Spirit or not.

People who have fragmented souls or personalities will also hear other voices. These may be demonic but usually they are another part of their fractured heart. This requires some process of inner healing where Jesus unites the fractured parts of the heart back to their adult core identity or original self.

After three years of drought, Elijah heard in the Spirit the sound of rain (1 Kings 18:41). He then prayed for rain until it came. However, Elijah struggled to hear God when he came under the fear of Jezebel. God spoke to him, not in the wind nor earthquake or fire, but through a gentle whisper (1 Kings 19:11-13). God speaks to us through His still, quiet voice as we open our hearts to Him.

Taste

The Psalmist says: *'Taste and see that the Lord is good'* (Psalm 34:8). Taste is a sense we don't use much in the spiritual realm but God can still speak to us through it. Scripture speaks about tasting the goodness of the Word of God as we eat and chew on it (Hebrews 6:4-5).

Nature

Another way God speaks to us is through nature and His creation. Words, feelings or impressions may enter my mind as I look at the beauty of His creation around me. Jesus spoke to His disciples figuratively with nature, as with the Shepherd and His sheep, the vine and the branches, the tree bearing fruit and so on.

God spoke to me through nature after I failed my final medical exam. I was disappointed and wanted to know why He allowed this after my hard work, so I walked outside in the pouring rain venting my feelings. After releasing all my frustrations and disappointment, I sat on a tree stump looking at some trees in the distance. My eyes caught view of an ugly, bare tree which had no fruit or leaves. Instantly the words came to me that this tree was like me, where I needed pruning in order to bear fruit. I had developed a pride, believing the lie that I could get through medicine without God's help. He allowed me to fail so He could humble me. I knew these thoughts were not my own thinking but were scriptural and from God.

God spoke to Jeremiah through the potter and the clay. He told him to go down to the potter's house. It was there He would speak to him (Jeremiah 18:1-10).

God can speak to us powerfully through nature if we are open to this. However, we must be careful not to interpret every natural thing we see as being a word from God. We simply need to be open to God's Spirit and discern when it is His Spirit speaking to us through nature, rather than trying to conjure something up ourselves. When it is a thought from God it will come effortlessly and we will sense the Spirit drawing our attention to something. God usually (but not always) will confirm what He is saying through His written word.

People

God can speak to us through people as they speak into our lives. When a spoken word stirs our spirit, it may be from God. People who I would have least expected to speak into my life have been used by God to speak words that have touched my spirit deeply. God also loves speaking to our hearts from the mouths of little children. He has used little children to speak or minister to my heart and spirit on many occasions.

His Messenger Angels

God may send His angels to deliver messages, like the angel Gabriel who appeared to Mary or the angel who appeared to John in the book of Revelation. Sometimes, God sends His angels in human form and only later do we realise (Hebrews 13:2).

When I worked in Uganda I struggled every time a child died, especially when I had been fighting for the child's life. My whole body would feel numb and I would want to stop what I was doing and head back to England. Each time this happened, I would encounter a healthy little Ugandan child who would just minister love and joy to my spirit and heart, by the radiance shining from their face. Then the child would disappear. It was as if God was sending a little healthy one to encourage me in my work. It always worked and the numbness lifted, enabling me to continue. I have no idea if some were angels but I would not be surprised if they were because they appeared at the right moment and non-verbally ministered to my spirit each time.

Impressions

Many times we have thoughts or impressions and need to discern if they are from our flesh, the devil or God. It is easier to accept a thought as being from God when we are in His Presence or sense His peace.

We may receive impressions when praying for others. They may mean nothing to us but mean everything to the person. When this occurs we should speak the thought or picture without saying *'thus says the Lord'*. Instead, we should let them make the decision if it is God or not.

Sometimes we may have a vague thought but it can be from God. We need to pursue it in prayer, asking God to confirm if it is from Him or our flesh. Sometimes, thoughts may be simple nudges from Him to do something. These may be nudges to give someone a call or go to a particular place. We shouldn't ignore them because we may be missing out on reaching out to someone. We need to ask Him to make us more sensitive to His little nudges- those random thoughts that come to our mind, for they may happen to be from Him!

Blockages to Hearing God

God is a God of relationship who loves to communicate with His children. There are different things that can block us from hearing Him. Being aware can help us get into the right mind and spirit to hear Him more clearly. Here are some things that may hinder us from hearing God.

Sin & Disobedience

David loved coming into God's presence and communing with Him, for he was a man after God's heart (1 Samuel 13:14). One of his prayers was this: *'Search me oh God and know my heart; test me and know my anxious thoughts. See if there is any offensive way in me'* (Psalm 139:23-24). David didn't want anything to get in the way of hearing God. So whenever he struggled to hear God, he would check if there was any sin in his heart.

When Saul inquired of the Lord if he should fight the Philistines, God didn't answer him. Saul immediately thought there must sin in the camp: *'So Saul asked God, "Shall I go down after the Philistines? Will You give them into Israel's hands?" But God did not answer him that day. Saul therefore said, "Come here, all you who are leaders of the army, and let us find out what sin has been committed today"'* (1 Samuel 14:37-38).

When we struggle to hear God it may be because we have allowed sin or disobedience to get in the way. Disobedience actually dulls our spirit to hearing Him. It is harder to hear someone when we choose to walk away from them. However, those who have clean hands and a pure heart will hear God (Psalm 24:3-4). Jesus said: *'Blessed are the pure in heart, for they will see God'* (Mathew 5:8). Impure or sinful thoughts will block us hearing God. If we want to hear God we need to turn from any sin or disobedience and choose to return to Him. He is always waiting for us to come back and be in continuous relationship with Him.

Negative Attitude

Negative attitudes are not of God. Hence, each time our hearts respond with a negative attitude we quench the Spirit of God in us. A negative attitude includes negative thoughts and feelings, or saying words that hurt others. Pride, jealousy, competition, judgment, anger (except righteous anger), victim mindset, gossip and criticism are all from our carnal nature. They quench God's Spirit in us. Again, we need to recognize this and get our hearts right before God and others where appropriate. False beliefs and lies, about our self and God, will prevent us hearing Him. We need to know His truth and deal with our negative thoughts so we can open our hearts again to hearing Him.

Stress & Anxiety

Stress or anxiety is a number one quencher of the Spirit of God. Fear is one of Satan's main strongholds that prevents us from hearing God or moving in His Spirit. It is hard to hear His Spirit when we carry fear, anxiety or stress. We need to deal with these by handing them over to God in exchange for His peace. It is easier to hear Him when we have His peace in our hearts (Philippians 4:6). His peace helps us hear His truth for each given situation, and to respond in the power of His Spirit.

The Lie that God Won't Speak

Some may struggle to hear God because they are living under a lie that He has no time for them or doesn't want to speak to them. Some have been told, 'What makes *you* think God speaks to you!!' This may be from a spirit of unbelief or insignificance. In some cases, it may be because our parents or siblings didn't give us the appropriate love or attention when needed. God has so much He wants to speak into our hearts and lives. This is where we need faith to believe this truth. God will listen to us every minute of the day and wants to tell us what is on His heart.

God speaks to everyone and not just to pastors or prophets. It's a lie to think we are not good enough for Him to speak to us. We are worthy for we are His children and our Heavenly Father wants to speak to His children. Like Samuel, we can say, '*Speak Lord, for your servant is listening*' and know that He does have something to say. We need to have faith He will speak to us and then be open to what He says.

Wanting to be in Control

It is hard to acknowledge God's will or hear Him speak on a certain issue where we want to be in control. This may be because we are afraid of what He might say and don't want to hear Him. This desire for control may be over choices like relationships, finances, homes, jobs or our future. Fear is a stronghold of the enemy. We need to surrender any fear to God and choose to put our trust in Him.

On one occasion I feared selling my home because I didn't want to sell it, so I didn't ask God if it was His will. Instead, I prayed He would provide tenants. When this wasn't happening, a friend prayed and sensed it may be right to sell my house. I realised I had to surrender my control and seek His will. I had not been able to hear Him because I had been blocking the answer by refusing to let go of my home.

Many times my logical reasoning has blocked me from hearing God. I have learnt to offer my own rational thoughts to God and then wait for His response for each problem or issue. God's thoughts are not our thoughts (Isaiah 55:8). As we surrender our thoughts to Him and give Him control in our lives, it becomes much easier to hear Him and obey His will.

Not Willing to Wait on God

Sometimes we may need to wait on God in order to hear Him speak. When we are busy or tired it is hard to focus on Him. Hence, He tells us to be still and know that He is God (Psalm 46:10). Sometimes we choose to be busy like Martha and allow distractions to block us from hearing God. He wants us to stop, look and listen as we choose to 'just be' in His Presence.

Sometimes God will speak to us at the last minute of the hour. He wants to see how much we will wait for Him and not be off in a rush. *How much do we want to hear Him?* Always wait for an answer and He will give it. Never be in a rush. The most amazing breakthroughs are when men and women have spent days or nights in prayer and fasting, seeking God and waiting on Him. David knew how to wait on the Lord: *'Wait for the Lord, be strong and take heart and wait for the Lord'* (Psalm 27:14).

Once when I was struggling to hear God at a particular time in my life, I decided to fast until He spoke to me. I was desperate to know His will in my life. On the third day of the fast, I suddenly became aware of His awesome Presence in my room. Joy started to flow through my heart and the despair and hopelessness lifted from me. I knew in my heart and spirit He was right with me, and was leading me into a new season with Him. It was as if He had opened a new door for me to walk through. This was the result of pressing in further through prayer and fasting.

Self-Focused

We struggle to hear God when we are absorbed with our own issues or thoughts. Without realising, we become self-focused and preoccupied with self, that we stop hearing Him. Self-pity or a victim mindset will block us hearing Him and is actually a sin. Our attention is on 'me' and 'my needs' or 'my rights' instead of being God-focused. This is actually a form of pride. The word pride has 'I' in the centre. God opposes the proud but gives grace to the humble (James 4:6): '*Humble yourselves, therefore, under God's almighty hand, that He may lift you up in due time. Cast all your anxiety on Him for He cares for you*' (1 Peter 5:5-6). As we take time to quieten ourselves before God, He will direct our paths and guide us with His peace.

Mind Block

Sometimes, there may be a spirit blocking our minds from hearing God, or a *spirit of mind-block*. This may be the result of past or present involvement with the occult, witchcraft, martial arts or freemasonry. Also, it may be the result of personal sin or it may have come down the bloodline as a result of the sins of our parents and forefathers. If so, then we can repent and take authority over any spirit of mind-block, and invite the Holy Spirit to unblock our minds and spirit so we may hear Him.

People may hear God before receiving Jesus in their hearts. God can influence people in governmental power though they may not know their thoughts are from Him. God can speak to us at any moment through any means. The most important thing is we learn to discern what is from our own thinking (or flesh), what is from the devil and what is from God. (More can be read on spiritual discernment in Volume 2).

END NOTES

[1]   Brother Lawrence; *Practice of the Presence of God.*
[2]   QAVAH (Hebrew 6960); *Strong's Exhaustive Expanded Concordance; Red Letter Edition (2001).*

5

Gifts & Anointing

We have different gifts according to the grace given us

Romans 12:6

Many believe the gifts and anointing are the same, whereas others believe they are quite different. Let us look at both in more detail.

Gifts of the Spirit

Most are aware the baptism of the Holy Spirit is a gift from God made available for all believers. However, Paul took this a step further and referred to the *gifts* of the Spirit being available for all *Spirit-filled* believers. The spiritual gifts are from the same Spirit and given as the Holy Spirit determines. *'There are different kinds of gifts but the same Spirit. Now to each one the manifestation of the Spirit is given for the common good. To one there is given through the Spirit the **word of wisdom**, to another the **word of knowledge** by means of the same Spirit, to another **faith** by the same Spirit, to another **gifts of healing** by that one Spirit, to another **miraculous powers**, to another **prophecy**, to another **distinguishing between spirits**, to another speaking in **different kinds of tongues** and to another, the **interpretation of tongues**. All these are works of the one and same Spirit and He gives them to each one, just as He determines'* (1

81

Corinthians 12:1-11). All of us are born with natural gifts and abilities, but the gifts referred to here are supernatural gifts given by the Spirit as He determines.

Many receive these gifts when baptized with the Holy Spirit or sometime later. A gift available for every Spirit-filled believer is the gift of speaking in tongues. A gift may be imparted either by someone who has the gift, through the laying on of hands, or directly by the Holy Spirit. Receiving a gift of the Spirit does not reflect maturity of character, since we usually receive them when we are immature or young in our spiritual growth. However, spiritual authority is required to exercise a gift, which we get from our relationship with God. There are different levels of authority depending on our personal depth of intimacy. All the gifts of the Spirit are available for each Spirit-filled believer, though some may be encouraged to use a certain gift. A gift is like receiving a present in a box. After we receive it, we need to take it out and use it, and we do this by faith.

Why do we Need Gifts?
God has given us the spiritual gifts to help us grow in the Spirit and to encourage and build each other up in the body of Christ. The gift of tongues is to build up our spirit (through prayer and worship) and enables us to pray in the Spirit for others. The gift of prophecy is mainly to build up the body of Christ (1 Corinthians 14:4-5), and also to prophecy or speak from God's heart to those who don't yet know Him.

Paul said: *'We have **different gifts, according to the grace given us.** If a man's gift is prophesying**, let him use it in proportion to his faith.** If it is serving, let him serve; if it is teaching, let him teach; if it is encouraging, let him encourage; if it is contributing to the needs of others, let him give generously; if it is in leadership, let him govern diligently'* (Romans 12:6-8). Gifts are given by God's grace, and we operate a gift according to our measure of faith and authority in Christ. Therefore, they are limited according to the proportion of faith and authority we carry.

Paul said that our callings and gifts are irrevocable. We will always have them, and even if we sin, they will not be taken from us (Romans 11:29). This is because the gift is part of our calling. There is the danger of having a gift but misusing it for selfish reasons or for financial gain. Just because we have a spiritual gift doesn't mean we will enter the Kingdom of heaven. It was freely given by grace to help build up the body of Christ. Jesus said not everyone who says to Him, 'Lord, Lord' will enter the kingdom of heaven, but only he who does God's will. *'Many will say to Me on that day, "Lord, Lord, did we not prophesy in Your name, and in Your name drive out demons and perform many miracles?" Then I will tell them plainly, "I never knew you. Away from Me, you evildoers!"'* (Matthew 7:21-23).

A gift is a particular manifestation of the Holy Spirit, freely given by the grace of God and used in proportion to our faith, to build up the body of Christ. It is therefore limited. However, it is also true to say, gifts may have various levels of anointing. Ten people with the same gift can operate with different levels of anointing, according to the level of power and authority they carry. This is because God increases His anointing the more we mature in our character and deepen our relationship with Him.

The level of authority we carry is dependent on the depth of our relationship with God. Though a gift is free, there is a price to pay if we want His anointing.

When we receive a gift, it is our responsibility to use it instead of putting it on the shelf. Paul reminded Timothy to fan into flame the gift of God given to him through the laying on of hands (2 Timothy 1:6). A gift is a bit like receiving a tool to help harvest God's Kingdom. The more we use it and learn from our mistakes, the more fruit we will bear in His Kingdom, and our Father may give us an upgrade.

Anointing of the Spirit

The anointing is the power and authority of the Spirit given to each Spirit-filled believer. The anointing we receive is not for our personal use but for the benefit of others, though we are empowered by His Spirit in the process. At different stages of our spiritual journey with God, He will increase His anointing. This is dependent on our hunger for Him and obedience to His will. His anointing comes as we spend more time soaking and resting in

His Presence. It is like an overflow or outpouring of His Spirit from simply being in His presence.

As I was meditating on God's grace and asking for more understanding, He gave me a picture. In the picture, I saw a person's natural strength. The person had strong, bulging muscles throughout their body, which represented their natural strength or flesh. Next, I saw them standing before Jesus and surrendering each part of their flesh to Him. Their flesh diminished as they lay down the various parts of their carnal nature. Each part of surrendered flesh represented a part of their carnal nature, such as the need to strive, need to achieve, need to be accepted, need to lead, need to defend, need to seek reward, need to take control, need to be heard, need to judge, and so forth. As each piece of carnal nature was surrendered, the size of the body began to diminish until it became miniscule, like the size of a mouse. This was the result of the flesh, bit by bit, being crucified. Next, I saw the Spirit of God come and make His home in this small body. Suddenly, the body began to increase in size as the Spirit took over and inhabited it. It became far larger than the natural body. It was huge, for it was full of God's Spirit. It was full of His grace, love, mercy, kindness, peace, generosity and so on. Then these words came: 'It is no longer I who live, but Christ who lives in me' (Galatians 2:20). As we surrender the areas of our flesh to God, He will exchange them with His supernatural strength and power. This is His grace. God is moving us from human effort to spiritual muscle.

I asked the Lord for further revelation concerning the difference between the gifts of the Spirit and anointing. Then one morning as I awoke, I had a picture of two identical looking wooden chests. Both appeared heavy, but one was twice the size of the other. I somehow knew in my spirit that I could lift the smaller box, but the larger box was too heavy to move. Straight away, the Spirit revealed these were the same gift but with different 'weights' of His anointing. In order to carry greater weights of the anointing, we need to develop our 'spiritual muscles'. Our muscles form as we develop the various fruits of the Spirit, which are the character and nature of God. It may be we need to develop more in areas such as faith, humility, grace, wisdom, compassion, and a servant heart, before we can carry the next weight or measure of anointing. If our spiritual muscles are weak, we will be unable to carry the heavier weight of anointing, for it will simply crush us. Only by dying to the different areas of our flesh can our spiritual muscles increase in strength and thus carry greater levels of His anointing. This is why His grace is a necessary requirement to walking in His anointing. Our spiritual strength is dependent on the level we walk in the grace of God. Much grace was upon the Apostles, enabling them to minister with such power and authority (Acts 4:33). Through humility, we realize that we can't do the things we are called to do in our own strength, but need to lean on the power and strength of Jesus. This is what it means to live by His grace (Romans 11:6).

After His resurrection, Jesus told the Apostles to wait for the promise His Father had given them. He said: *'You will receive power when the Holy Spirit comes on you'* (Acts 1:8). It was in a certain place at a certain time when they were clothed with power from on high. They had already received power and authority to heal the sick and cast out demons during their intimate three-and-a-half-years with Jesus, but this was different. They were being prepared to receive greater levels of power and authority. They received heavier weights or mantles to go and disciple nations and take over the work Jesus had been doing.

God gives mantles to His sons and daughters who have said 'yes' to a higher calling and willingly paid a sacrificial price. Mantles are for those whom the Lord appoints to train and equip the body of Christ. Great grace and humility are required to carry such mantles of power and authority.

Over the years, I have noticed the Lord release more power and authority after spending considerable time in His presence. This involves learning His ways and receiving discipline where needed (2 Timothy 3:16). The higher we are willing to climb up the mountain with God, then the less of 'self' because this requires laying down our carnal nature. The less of self creates greater capacity to carry more of His presence and anointing.

A Gifted Teacher and One Who Teaches With an Anointing

There is a difference between a gifted teacher and one who teaches with an anointing. A gifted teacher is someone who has the ability to teach well. However, someone who teaches with an anointing will be able to speak or minister to our spirit, because each word they speak carries power and authority. I have sat in meetings where the teaching has been good but lacked the anointing of the Spirit. Likewise, I have been in meetings where I have felt such a presence of God flow from the mouth of the anointed speaker, their words have ministered with power directly to my spirit.

An anointed person brings fresh revelation from the mouth of God. Instead of just renewed fact, they carry the life and power of God's Spirit. I believe God no longer wants us to speak facts *about* Him and His Kingdom, but rather let His Spirit flow with power *through* our mouth, so His Spirit can minister directly to the hearts of His people. Jesus, the living Word, wants to come and inhabit our spiritual bodies, so He may commune with us and through us to others.

Paul said: '*My message and my preaching were not with **wise and persuasive words**, but with a demonstration of **the Spirit's power** [dunamis], so that your faith may **not rest on men's wisdom, but on God's power [dunamis]**'* (1 Corinthians 2:4-5). The more we die to our flesh, the more we can speak what we hear Him speak and do what we see Him do. This comes through the power of His Spirit abiding in us.

Price Behind the Anointing

We must not forget that the gifts and anointing are given by grace. However, there is usually a price behind the anointing.

Many who want other people's anointing are unaware of the price behind the anointing[1] and the challenges that come with it. God desires to release His anointing on all His children, but usually after passing tests, just as Jesus did in the desert. If we want to be vessels that carry His anointing, then we must be willing to let Him test and circumcise our hearts. This will include undergoing death to reputation, death to man-made theology and religion, death to fears and control, death to all forms of pride (anything including self), and like David, having a passionate heart that seeks after God's own heart.

Those who carry an anointing need to be able to deal with opposition, for the enemy is out to kill, steal and destroy God's anointed ones. This includes dealing with jealousy or 'hate mail', false accusations, being misinterpreted, and slandered. Or they may face the pressures and temptations that come with success or fame including false friendships, sexual temptations, spiritual pride or lust for money and power. Either way, our hearts need to be tested and refined, so we can be spiritually immune to such temptations or attacks. This involves a lifestyle of seeking His presence as we regularly offer ourselves to Him as broken bread and poured out wine.

Minister In His Presence

Gifts are Kingdom tools to help build up, heal and encourage the body of Christ. I believe the gifts are to help get us started on our journey of sonship with God. However, there is a risk of developing pride and arrogance with the gifts of the Spirit. This is because our character is still immature, and we are tempted to think that the healing is due to *our* power and gifting. Only as we grow more in our personal relationship with God, will we develop in character and gradually change our perspective from being self-focused to God-focused. We will learn to see how it is all about Him and *His power* and not about us. Instead of God assisting us, we become the ones assisting Him.

After serving on the mission field for seven years, God called me back to England. The first thing He said was to no longer focus on ministry, but Him. I was entering a new season where He was calling me to pursue His presence. He was revealing how greater anointing flows from those who walk in His presence. This required a complete shift in mindset, for my heart and mind were to focus on Him and not my work or ministry. This required learning to walk in His grace and humility. Someone said, *'Humility is not thinking less of yourself; it's thinking of yourself less.'*

The Lord gives us the gifts of the Spirit to encourage us when we are still young in faith. However, as we mature in sonship, He will move us on from relying on the gifts to operating in His presence. Gifts given through the laying on of hands were considered to be *elemental* or foundational, as was raising the dead (Hebrews 6:1-2). However, His presence is for those who pursue Him. Our ultimate goal is to pursue a life of abiding in His presence. Instead of operating from a *word* of knowledge or *word* of wisdom as comes with the gifts, we are to co-labour with the *Spirit* of knowledge and the *Spirit of* wisdom and revelation, as we pursue the *full measure* of son-ship. Maturing in spiritual sonship is about developing in the *fullness* of sonship. This is by moving on from using the gifts to walking in His manifest presence. We no longer focus on just the gifts but the Giver Himself, as we discover how to co-labour with His Spirit.

END NOTES
[1] Austin, Jill; *In the Hands of the Master Potter: The Price Behind the Anointing* (Master Potter Ministries; *www.lastdaysministries.org*)

6

Spirit, Soul & Body

*Let us purify ourselves from everything
that contaminates body and spirit*

2 Corinthians 7:1

God created us with a spirit, soul and body, so we could love the Lord our God with *all* our heart, soul, mind and strength. The Passion Translation reads: *'You are to love the Lord Yahweh, your God, with every passion of your heart, with all the energy of your being, with every thought that is within you and with all your strength,'* (Mark 12:30, Luke 10:27, Mathew 22:37, Deuteronomy 6:5).

True worship is worshipping God with our whole being. Paul said to offer our bodies as living sacrifices, holy and pleasing to God. This is our spiritual act of worship (Romans 12:2).

Spirit, Soul and Body

One of the divine truths is we were created to be *spirit beings.* Adam and Eve were spirit beings before they sinned. As a result of sin, they lost their immortality and became mortal beings. Suddenly, they became aware of their flesh, hence covered themselves with fig leaves. Since then, our flesh has been ruling our spirit and there has been an ongoing battle between our flesh and spirit.

Jesus came to restore our spirit back to God, so our spirit could once more take mastery over our flesh. He said: *'The Spirit gives life; the flesh counts for nothing,'* (John 6:63). When the disciples were unable to stay awake for one hour with Jesus, He said: *'The Spirit is willing but the flesh is weak,'* (Matthew 26:41).

Our spirit is supposed to rule our flesh and house our body, and not the other way around. When we are in a deep place of communion with God, we are no longer aware of our body. In some cases, our body may appear transparent and glow radiantly as we intimately engage in the glory-presence of the Lord. This is because our spirit being has expanded beyond our body. Moses face shone brilliantly every time he was in the glory-presence of God. Paul mentioned the bodies changing and becoming like His glorious body (Philippians 3:21).

Paul said we have a natural body and a spiritual body (1 Corinthians 15:44-45). He didn't know if his body was with him or not, when his spirit was caught up in paradise with God (2 Corinthians 12:2). Our bodies are living temples or spiritual dwellings for God's Spirit to come and rest. We were created to be living tabernacles to house His presence (1 Corinthians 3:16). *'And in Him you too are being built together to become a dwelling in which God lives by His Spirit,'* (Ephesians 2:22).

When we refer to our 'body, soul and spirit' in that order, we are in effect declaring our bodies to be greater than our spirit. However, we are spirit beings that house a body, because our body is mortal but our spirit is eternal. Paul knew this when he said to the Thessalonians: *'May God Himself, the God of peace, sanctify you through and through. May your **whole spirit, soul and body** be kept blameless as the coming of the Lord Jesus Christ,'* (1 Thessalonians 5:23). Paul saw the spirit as having rulership over the soul and body. This is because the soul and body form our flesh, and Jesus said we are not to live by the flesh but the spirit. This means our spirit is to have mastery over our flesh. One of the ways we can do this is through fasting from things of the flesh. Biblically speaking, fasting was usually from food, because food feeds the flesh. However, we may fast from other things, such as alcohol, sex, TV, social media or negative thinking.

Something happened when I started to daily surrender my flesh (body and soul) to my spirit, and command my spirit to come under the influence of the Holy Spirit. When I had a flu-like illness that drained all energy from my body, my spirit remained unaffected. My spirit could easily rise above the illness and worship God, though my flesh felt weak. Previously, my spirit would feel affected whenever my body was fighting an infection. This time was different, because it was as if my spirit wasn't affected. Then I realized it was because my spirit now ruled over my flesh and wasn't under the influence of it anymore. This was a radical breakthrough. It is a daily choice to surrender our flesh to our spirit and our spirit to the Holy Spirit, so we live by the influence of His Spirit and no longer by our flesh. This enables us to live a Spirit-led life, instead of a flesh-led life (Zechariah 4:6).

Our *body* forms our physical makeup and this includes our five natural senses; sight, smell, hearing, touch and taste. Our natural senses feed information to our soul.

Our *soul* consists of our mind (including intellect and imagination), will (or choices) and emotions (or feelings). Many use the word 'soul' when referring to the spirit, though they are different. However, the word for soul in scriptures may refer to the heart. This is because the heart and mind are inter-connected, since they influence each other. What we think in the mind will influence how we feel in the heart and vice versa. Our soul is the bridge between the physical world and spiritual world.

Our *spirit* is our inner being and comes alive when we are born-again, or encounter the Holy Spirit. It doesn't need to sleep when our body and soul sleeps, because it is immortal. Hence, our spirit can engage with God while our body and soul rests at night. We were created to commune with God, Spirit to spirit. Our spirit comprehends more than our soul. Hence, it may be hard to explain in human words what we encounter or experience with our spirit.

Our body, soul and spirit may each become defiled as a result of sin and demonic spirits. Hence, Paul said: '*Let us purify ourselves from everything that contaminates body and spirit,*' (2 Corinthians 7:1). When people inflict curses or other forms of witchcraft, it may affect our body, soul and spirit. Curses, witchcraft and demonic spirits may be the influences behind ill health, including mental and spiritual affliction.

The battle is real, because the enemy tries to come against God's people through sicknesses, temptations, fears, sexual sins and so on. Hence, we need to regularly cleanse and sanctify our spirit, soul and body with the blood of Jesus. This includes renouncing ungodly or unclean spirits and renewing our minds daily. Paul addresses such matters: '*May your **whole** being, spirit, soul and body, be kept blameless,*' (1 Thessalonians 5:23) .

Biblical References to Heart, Soul and Spirit

It is interesting that the words used for heart and soul, have similar meanings. However, the word for 'heart' is used more when referring to our emotions or passions, and the word for soul is used more when referring to our minds or thoughts.

Heart
The Hebrew word '*Leb*'[1] or '*Lebab*' may be the word used when referring to *the soul, mind, emotions, will and inner being.*
The Greek word '*Kardia*'[2] is where we get the word 'cardiac' and means heart. This can be used when referring to *thoughts, feelings and the broken-hearted.* So the word for heart in the Bible is used for emotions as well as our will, minds and thoughts. Hence, it can refer to the soul.

Soul
The Greek word for soul is '*Psyche*' [3] and means 'breath' or 'spirit'. However, it is also used to refer to the 'mind'. This is where we get the word 'psychology' meaning study of the mind. The Hebrew equivalent is '*Nephesh*' [4] and also means 'breath' but in relation to humans or creatures breathing.

Spirit
The Hebrew word for spirit is '*Ruwach*'[5] and refers to the 'wind', 'breath' and 'Spirit' of God. The Greek is '*Pneuma*'[6] where we get the medical words for lungs, like '*Pneumonia*'. This is used when referring to our 'spirit', or the breath of God and the Holy Spirit.

Influences on the Human Spirit, Soul & Body

Demonic spirits	**HUMAN SPIRIT**	*Holy Spirit*
Spirit of death Spirit of deception Spirit of fears/lies Occult/witchcraft	⇩	Revelation/Truth Seven Spirits(Is 11:2) Fruit of Spirit Gifts of Spirit
Selfishness Fear/Control Doubt/Unbelief Unforgiveness Anger/hate Pride/rebellion Negative mindset Sexual Sin Rejection Judge/Criticise Jealousy Orphan heart	**SOUL /HEART** MIND WILL EMOTION *Intellect Choices Feelings* *Imagination* Fight Flight Freeze ⇩	Truth/discernment Love/ generous Christ-like mind Forgiveness/mercy Repentance/Grace Faith/obedience Humility/servant Purity/transparent Worship/prayer Surrender Belonging/Identity Sonship heart
Diseases Mental health Breakdown Disabilities Gen' illness	**BODY** *Hear, see, smell, feel, taste* Speak Do	Healthy Undivided heart Youthful Sound mind

The diagram is simply an outline to explain how the human spirit has influence over our soul, which in turn has influence over our body. As mentioned above, the soul is a bridge between the spiritual and physical world. The spirit realm (whether it is demonic spirits or the Holy Spirit) can directly affect our spirit, soul and body. When the Holy Spirit influences our spirit and soul, we bear Kingdom fruit and take on more of a Godly attitude and character. Likewise, when demonic spirits influence our spirit and soul, we will bear ungodly fruit and demonic strongholds. The body is affected by the soul and spirit. The words we think and what we speak over our body will affect our health, for there is power in the tongue. We can bless or curse, and speak life or death (Proverbs 18:21, James 3:9-10).

Blessings & Curses

Blessings and curses can affect our spirit, soul and body. Hence, that is why we are no longer to curse, but to bless. Jesus said: '*Love your enemies. Do good to those who hate you, bless those who curse you, pray for those who mistreat you,*' (Luke 6:28). Our tongue is a powerful weapon that can work for us or against us, when we choose to bless or curse respectively. Without realizing, we may curse our self and others, when we speak or think negative words, or become critical towards others or our self.

Charles Capps[7] has written a booklet on the power behind blessing your body and I believe it works. Our body cells and organs respond to the authority in our voice. God has given us authority over our bodies. That is another reason why our flesh is to come under our spirit.

Arthur Burk has written a book and audio with Sylvia Gunter on 'Blessing Your Spirit'[8] (www.theslg.com). I recommend this audio for it will minister truth to your spirit. The spoken words are from scriptures, but instead of processing them in your soul or mind, they are received in your spirit man or inner being. Hence, your spirit is blessed. This is ministering from God's Spirit to your spirit.

Sometimes, I may minister to a person's spirit by speaking directly to their spirit. This may be with the eyes closed or open. However, as we look intentionally in a person's eyes, we communicate to their soul and spirit. This is because the eyes are the gateway to the soul. The way God originally designed us to communicate was spirit to spirit. This was before the fall and rebellion of man, when different languages came about. Hence, when God downloads Kingdom revelations or Heavenly visions, words are not enough to express what we have seen or experienced in our spirit being.

Flesh versus Spirit

As already mentioned, our 'flesh' is our body and soul. Our soul governs our body. My body responds to my thoughts (conscious or sub-conscious) to carry out a function. However, we can be influenced by the world, flesh, devil or God's Spirit. For example, pride, selfishness, unforgiveness, jealousy, witchcraft, hatred, sexual sin and so forth are part of our soulish or earthly nature (Galatians 5:17-25, Colossians 3). These come from living under the influences of the world, flesh and devil. Hence, our battle in life is constantly between our 'flesh' and 'spirit,' as our flesh rebels against the Spirit of God (John 6:63).

Since our body, soul and spirit are connected, they influence one another. If we have a physical ailment, such as an injury or infection, then this affects our spiritual and emotional wellbeing. Likewise, if we have a prime emotional issue such as fear, emotional pain or stress, it can affect our physical health and well being. John touched on this when he said: '*I pray that you may enjoy good health and that all may go well with you, even as your soul is getting along well,*' (3 John verse 2).

Therefore, it is important to consider spiritual or emotional causes to physical symptoms and not see them as separate. I have seen people with injuries where there was a spirit of witchcraft behind the injury. Accidents and sickness can be the result of curses or spiritual attack. The Lord is our Great Physician who knows what is going on in everyone. All we need to do is ask Him what is behind the symptom or illness. Once we address the root, we can begin to see healing and wholeness restored.

Medicine plays a vital part in health, as I experienced during my years as a medical doctor. However, we need wisdom and discernment when to take medicines and when to address a possible emotional or spiritual root.

There can be a misconception when people think they are 'resistant' to treatment or medication doesn't work. It could simply be that the symptoms need to be 'spiritually' or 'emotionally' diagnosed and treated first. It would be cost effective if we were to address the spiritual and emotional roots to our health prior to giving out any drugs or performing unnecessary tests or operations.

Jesus physically healed many when He said, '*Your sins are forgiven*', but He also said, '*Sin no more!*' After Jesus healed the invalid He told him to stop sinning or something worse may happen (John 5:14). He healed all who came to Him and all who touched Him (Acts 10:38, Mathew 8:16, 14:36). As it says in Psalm 103:3, the Lord *forgives all* your sin *and heals all* your diseases. He came to destroy the works of the devil and that includes healing and restoring us back to full health (John 10:10, 1 John 3:8). He came to restore our soul: our mind, will and emotions (Psalm 23:3). As we set our hearts and minds on things above and not on earthly things, then Christ's peace can rule in our hearts (Colossians 3:1-2, 15). Here, Paul was referring to our soul (heart and mind) coming under the rulership of God's Spirit (His peace).

Spiritual Roots

Different things occurring in our lives can have a negative effect on our health. Hence, we need a Counselor, the Holy Spirit, to reveal the spiritual roots or underlying causes to the symptoms. Some roots may go back to childhood or the moment of conception. Other roots may involve the sins passed down the bloodline as a result of the sins and curses from our parents and forefathers.

As a children's doctor, I would come across various cases where the real problem was the child's emotional or spiritual needs not being met. A mother brought me her three year old girl who developed acute urine retention. She had failed to pass urine for over forty-eight hours. On examination, her bladder was tender and grossly enlarged. On further questioning, I discovered the parents had just moved home forty-eight hours ago and had neglected their child during this time. It then became obvious that the little girl was seeking attention or trying to feel in control. I smiled at the little girl and gave her a choice. She could voluntarily pass urine in a bowl or I could catheterise her. When she saw the catheter, she opted for the bowl. Within seconds, she voluntarily emptied her bladder. The mother was embarrassed, yet relieved when she realized the root to the problem.

During my time in Africa when I happened to be teaching hospital staff on spiritual roots to sickness and disease, most of those present had chronic symptoms that hadn't responded to medicines or surgery. However, the symptoms responded once the spiritual roots were addressed through prayer. There were two senior nurses with chronic abdominal symptoms. One had undergone a major surgical operation with no improvement, whilst the other had undergone two major operations with little improvement. Their level of pain was unchanged. A pastor in the team prayed for one of the nurses, and as he took authority over the sickness, she started to cry and let out a loud shrieking noise. She then testified to a spirit leaving her body and the pain instantly left with it. She had no idea it was demonic in origin, but was relieved to be healed and set free.

The other senior nurse had chronic lower abdominal pain in the region of her feminine organs. I felt led to ask her if she had any issues as a mother, wife or sister. She started to cry and said yes. After listening to her issues, she was willing to forgive those who had hurt or disappointed her, and repent where she herself was guilty. Then we broke off any curses spoken over her (as a mother, wife or sister) and commanded the spirit of infirmity to leave. At the end, we asked God to bless her feminine organs, and blessed her as a mother, wife and sister. With tears of joy in her eyes, she declared her pain had gone.

God instantly heals when there is a great outpouring of His presence. However, He may choose to heal us through other approaches, because He wants to bring our attention to the roots of the problem. We are then the wiser by knowing the cause and can prevent it from recurring.

There was a lady who had inflammatory bowel disease and though she was on medication, she still had recurrent flare ups. After a friend gave her my book, *'Healing God's Way,'* she thought there may be a spiritual root to her illness. After questioning, it became evident each flare up was the result of a stressful situation. Through prayer, the Holy Spirit revealed the hidden roots of anger and unforgiveness. Once these were addressed, her symptoms started to resolve over the next few weeks. Six months later, she had another episode but this time she was able to recognize and deal with the roots to her stress instead of internalizing it. As a result, the symptoms resolved. She can now see how her bowel symptoms were simply an external manifestation of her inner spiritual and emotional stress.

Memory Cells

An interesting fact is that the spirit, soul and body each have memory cells. There is scientific evidence that reveals we have memory cells throughout our whole being. We have what is known as; *'cognitive'*, *'emotion'*, *'body'* and *'spirit'* memory. The cognitive (or conscious mind) and emotion memory can be seen as memory cells in our soul.

Cognitive Memory is the memory in the conscious or intellectual part of our brain and was previously thought to be on the left side of the brain in a right-handed person. However, recent studies believe cognitive memory is on both sides of the brain. This is the memory we use to study and learn data, store and recall facts and verbally process information. Hence, this is the factual or intellectual memory we use to access information for daily life.

Emotion Memory is the memory formed in the subconscious part of the brain, and was previously thought to be on the opposite side of the brain to the cognitive. Most of us have good and bad emotion memories. Painful emotion memories are usually locked or hidden somewhere in the subconscious area of our brain, for we may not want our conscious functioning part of the brain, to have access to these memories. This is why people may struggle to remember things in their childhood, because the painful memory is blocked or suppressed. Our conscious part, which is our daily functioning part of the brain, doesn't want to access or remember the painful emotions.

Studies have shown how emotion memory is stored in a structure known as the *amygdala*. The amygdala is an almond shaped pair of neurones, located on the medial (or inner) aspect of the temporal lobes. Hence, one is on both the right and left side. It is the main area where our negative and positive emotions are processed, especially fear and joy. Negative emotions include fear, anxiety and anger, and positive emotions include love, excitement and joy. The *amygdala* also processes decision-making. The *amygdala* works closely with the *hippocampus* and this stores our long and short-term memory.

Body Memory also known as cellular memory, is believed in some circles but not in others. However, body memory was noticed in a person who received a heart transplant. After the transplant, the person started to have flashback memories of a murder scene. It turned out the donated organ came from someone who was murdered. When they shared these intrusive memories with the police, it helped the police find the murderer. These flashback memories were the result of cellular memory stored in the heart organ. Plants don't have a brain or spirit, yet they probably have some sort of 'cellular memory' in order to divide and reproduce.

A lady came to see me after she developed a discomfort in her lower abdomen around her feminine organs. Her symptoms started after she received a word of knowledge, that God wanted to heal her of her childhood abuse. Her doctor tested her symptoms but could find nothing wrong. It appeared her symptoms were coming from the trauma stored in her body memory cells. After she received cleansing and healing in her body, soul and spirit, including the cleansing of the memory in her body cells, her symptoms instantly disappeared.

Whenever we receive donated blood or a donated organ, it is wise to cleanse it from any unclean spirits or foreign memory in the cells. We can erase any cellular memory and unclean spirits by cleansing it with the blood of Jesus. Scripture refers to memory cells in our body, in the case where God spoke about Cain murdering his brother Abel: '*What have you done? Listen! Your brother's blood cries out to me from the ground,*' (Genesis 4:10).

Spirit Memory is the memory retained by our spirit. Our spirit memory is helpful for accessing information especially during our time in the womb and the first few years of life. During the early stages of growth whilst the brain is still developing, the spirit memory is useful to recall painful memories.

I happened to be attending an event at Catch The Fire in Toronto, when the guest speaker asked the Holy Spirit to reveal to the audience any trauma in their first few years of life. To my surprise, I was taken back to being in the womb. It was the time I was about to be delivered and I saw myself getting stuck in this dark tunnel. I suddenly felt fearful, so I prayed and invited Jesus to the scene. Then I saw myself being pulled back and now there was white light all around me. My fear left as I felt the presence of God with me. This is an example of how the spirit memory can be useful during inner healing.

Some people have had 'out of body' experiences, where their spirit has left their body and then re-entered the body. Paul experienced this when he was taken to paradise, and didn't know if his spirit was still in the body or not (2 Corinthians 12:2). Spirit memory can recall supernatural experiences in the heavenly realms, like Paul when he was in paradise, and be extremely helpful during the healing of hearts.

So memory is stored in the cells of our body, cognitive mind, emotion and spirit. This is helpful when dealing with the healing of memories, especially with regards to traumas.

END NOTES:

[1] Leb/Lebab (Hebrew 3820 +3824); *Strong's Expanded Exhaustive Concordance, Red Letter Edition (2001)*
[2] Kardia (Greek 2588); *Strong's Expanded Exhaustive Concordance, Red Letter Edition (2001)*
[3] Psyche (Greek 5590); *Strong's Expanded Exhaustive Concordance, Red Letter Edition (2001)*
[4] Nephesh(Hebrew 5315); *Strong's Exhaustive Concordance, Red Letter Edition (2001)*
[5] Ruwach (Hebrew 7307); *Strong's Exhaustive Concordance, Red Letter Edition (2001)*
[6] Pneuma (Greek 4151); *Strong's Exhaustive Concordance, Red Letter Edition (2001)*
[7] Capps, Charles; *God's Creative Power For Healing (1991)*
[8] Burk, Arthur; *Blessing Your Spirit (2005)*

7

Spiritual History

The churches will know that I am He who searches hearts and minds

Revelation 2:23

A medical history taken by doctors collects relevant information from the patient for making a diagnosis. Likewise, a spiritual history can help when looking for underlying spiritual and emotional roots to symptoms or chronic issues. This is especially useful if someone hasn't responded to medicines or basic prayer.

I found myself asking people, *'What happened around the time you developed your problem?'* In the majority of cases, there was a trauma, emotional crisis, stressful season, or someone they needed to forgive. Many were unaware of the link between their physical symptoms, and their emotions and spirit.

Here are some questions we may ask that is similar to a medical history, but from a spiritual perspective.

Presenting Issue or Symptoms

Why has the Person Come for Prayer Ministry?
Sometimes the person is aware of the issue, such as self-hate or rejection, and other times they present with the symptom, such as

chronic body pain, rash, headaches, chronic cough, stiff shoulder, not wanting to live, or other issues. The symptom may be the manifestation of a deeper issue, or the fruit of the root.

History of Symptoms

When did the Problem Start?
It is important to know how long the symptoms have been happening. For some, it may be something acute or recent. For others, it may be a recurring issue. Usually, recurring issues will have a trigger. If so, what triggered the symptoms to return? For example, a person may have repeated episodes of acid reflux or gastritis, triggered every time there is stress in their marriage.

What Happened Around this Time?
Usually, some crisis or negative experience may have occurred around the time the symptoms started. This may be with work, a relationship, or a stressful/traumatic event.

Is there someone they may need to forgive? This may be evident in the information given, but usually the person isn't aware of anyone they may need to forgive. In some cases the person may have to forgive themselves, or deal with the feeling of disappointment and resentment towards God.

There was a lady who asked me to pray for her arthritic legs. So I asked her what happened around the time the pain started, and if there was someone she needed to forgive. Suddenly, the person remembered she had an argument with her mother-in-law and her symptoms started after this. Bitterness and unforgiveness had erupted and been the root behind her pain. The moment she forgave her mother-in-law, and repented of her own negative thoughts and emotions, the pain disappeared and she was healed from the arthritis.

A woman asked for prayer for the pain in her lower leg. When asked if there was anyone she needed to forgive, she immediately said yes. Tears came in her eyes as she forgave the person. When she tested her calf, the pain had gone.

Is there an Entry Point?

Sometimes, the person may or may not know when the problem started, or if there was an entry point when the symptoms began. In this case, ask the Holy Spirit during prayer, to shine His light on when it all started. *'The lamp of the Lord searches the spirit of a man; it searches out his innermost being'* (Proverbs 20:27). A memory may come back as the Holy Spirit reveals when it started. For example, a person with a fear of crowds may have had a negative experience of feeling crushed when young. Or a person who hates men may have been abused by a man.

Any other Associated Symptoms or Issues?

Sometimes, an issue may be linked to a cluster or group of other symptoms or issues, and these may need addressing. For example, unforgiveness is often linked to hatred, jealousy, judgement, resentment and bitterness. Or rejection may be linked to fear of man, low self-esteem, self-pity, self-hate, feeling not good enough, failure, and perfectionism. Hence, each of these may need addressing to see complete healing and freedom. It is a bit like a net where all the linked threads may need unhooking before the person is completely free. Or it may be compared to a tree with various roots, where each root may need attention before the main trunk can be uprooted.

Ungodly Vows, Covenants or Curses

Many people unconsciously make vows like, 'I will never...' or ' I will always...' especially when feeling hurt, wounded, angry or unforgiving. What we speak carries power. Hence, ungodly vows have to be renounced and broken.

Likewise, people may curse themselves or others through negative words. For example, 'I (you) am at fault and to blame. I am (you are) a failure. I am (you are) unloved. I am (you are) not liked or wanted. I am (you are) going to die'. And the list of negative words goes on. Curses also need to be broken for there is power in what we speak, whether to ourselves or others.

One lady suddenly lost her hearing and accepted she was deaf and probably needed a hearing aid. I questioned what had happened and asked if any cursed words had been spoken to her. Her husband had been calling her a deaf so and so, and she had accepted these cursed words. She repented of accepting the words and forgave her husband for what he said. We broke the curse on her ears in Jesus' name and I blessed her ears to hear again. Her hearing was instantly restored to what it was before.

Covenants are life-long promises made consciously or unconsciously. People who practice in the occult may have dedicated children to Satan through making covenants. Some African cultures dedicate their children to the ancestral spirits, for this is part of their traditional beliefs. In effect, the children are coming under a covenant with death, and this needs to be repented and broken. Covenants may occur through trade deals or business agreements. If these were ungodly trade deals, then they can be repented of and broken. Ungodly covenants can be binding and may keep a person in bondage.

Family History

Has the Issue or Problem been in the Family?

When parents and grandparents have suffered with the same sickness or problems, it usually means there is a familial or generational spirit behind the issue. Familial spirits appear normal, because you are used to seeing them in the family. Control, fear, anger, sexual sin, divorce, heart disease, specific illnesses, alcohol issues, freemasonry, or basically anything can be passed down the bloodline. Hence, each generational sin needs repentance and cleansing from the maternal and paternal bloodline.

All of us have sins passed down the bloodline from our forefathers. We have inherited good things from our parents and also bad or ungodly things. Some we may know and others we don't. The Holy Spirit can highlight any sin that needs cleansing from our bloodline. It is good practice to pray for the cleansing of the bloodline when dealing with any sickness, issue or sin.

A lady asked for a bunion on her foot to be healed. She said her mother had the same problem. So she forgave her mother and repented of any sin linked to the bunion in her family line. Curses come with generational sins, so we broke the curse and blessed her foot. Her bunion started to shrink as she felt the pressure ease immediately in her shoe.

Unhealthy Relationships or Soul-ties

An unhealthy soul-tie forms in any unhealthy relationship. This may be between colleagues, relatives, work relationships, church relationships and so on. Having a soul-tie is like feeling emotionally or spiritually 'pulled' by someone, and an obligation to do things for this person or under the influence of this person. It is an unhealthy yoke to someone. When soul-ties are broken people can feel free to be themselves again.

All sexual relationships form soul-ties. Hence, previous soul-ties, outside of a present healthy marriage, usually have to be broken in order to be spiritually set free from any previous sexual relationships.

Past Ministry

Has the Person Already Received Ministry?
If the person has already received ministry, then did it help? Or why didn't it help? What were the blockages during the ministry? It is good to know what level of ministry someone has received and discern if they need any more. Sometimes, the person may need to be encouraged to take responsibility for their health or issues, instead of going from one person to another. Or they may have had some ministry but a deeper level of healing may be required. Discernment is required as to what needs doing next.

Medication

Are they on any medication?
This doesn't have to be discussed unless relevant. Some may ask if they need to continue with their medication after receiving

ministry. The person must always check with their doctor concerning any prescribed medication, especially those on life saving medication or treatment for mental health issues. If a person is healed they should see their doctor to further discuss their medication. This is a great opportunity to testify God's healing to their doctor.

Addictions

People usually speak about their addiction if they are seeking ministry for this. There are many addictions such as alcohol, drugs, sex, pornography, TV, Facebook or anything you feel you can't live without. Addictions feed the cravings of the flesh and may cover up or numb the pain. There may be underlying roots such as wounded emotions, feeling unloved, or ongoing issues that need to be addressed.

Occult History

Has the person been involved in any occult activity including freemasonry? Or is there a family history of involvement with the occult? Do they have 'charms' or 'objects' like crystals, or anything else that may have evil spirits attached? This may be a relevant question for ongoing symptoms that haven't responded to first line prayer. A person who has been involved in the occult may struggle with ill health, ongoing demonic torment, or blockages in their relationship with God. Also, if anyone has possession of any good luck 'charms' or 'crystals' or 'fetishes' or any demonic looking objects, then these may block the healing or can make a person feel worse. They should be removed and ideally destroyed so no-one else is influenced by them.

I saw an African teenager who looked oppressed but was open for prayer. His eyes looked 'dark' spiritually speaking, as if he had been involved in witchcraft or the occult. When I asked if he had been involved, he admitted he had a voodoo doll and carried it with him. He repented of this and was willing to destroy it. He renounced the demonic spirits and then invited Jesus in to his heart. Suddenly, his countenance changed. He was now smiling as the oppressive spirit had lifted.

Abuse

Usually, a person will volunteer information if there has been any past or present abuse. I do not usually ask unless prompted by the Spirit, since this is a delicate area and the person may not be ready to disclose such information. The person may not want to speak about it unless they feel safe or the Spirit prompts them to do so. However, if the person has already had ministry, then they may feel they can discuss it more freely.

These questions are to help tease out the roots or underlying issues to a person's symptoms. They are not intended to be used in a methodical manner, like ticking boxes. They are to simply help provide questions that may reveal the roots to the symptoms. The main thing is to be led by the Spirit so things are asked and addressed as needed. The Spirit may give words of knowledge and wisdom concerning areas that require special attention. Hence, spiritual discernment is required to deal with most issues, because the person may focus on one area, when the main root for the problem is in a different area.

8

Roots to Symptoms

A tree is recognised by its fruit

Matthew 12:34

Behind the majority of chronic or ongoing health issues, there is probably a spiritual or emotional root. Henry W. Wright believes around eighty percent of the people he sees with chronic symptoms have spiritual roots.[1] I was ignorant of this whilst working as a hospital doctor in England, until the Lord called me to Africa. The majority of the sicknesses and illnesses I encountered had an emotional or spiritual root that required prayer ministry. The symptoms were real and in some ways debilitating, even when the tests came back normal. However, the symptoms usually disappeared once the roots to the sickness were addressed. In cases where people received both prayer and medication, healing was noted to be quicker compared to those who didn't receive prayer.

This is not to say that every sickness or disease has a spiritual or emotional root. Accidents or infections may occur that require the appropriate medical treatment. Even the prophet Isaiah referred to using a poultice of figs to treat an ailment (2 Kings 20:7)

I saw a teenage boy of another faith who had a productive cough and crackles on his chest. This was an obvious clinical chest infection. I prayed for him and then gave him antibiotics. However, after prayer, he looked me straight in the eyes and refused the antibiotics. He said his chest was completely healed. He seriously wanted to pursue the God he had just encountered, for the rest of His life.

There was another case of a lady who was HIV infected and came to me for antibiotics for her chest infection. I felt strongly in my spirit to pray for her before giving her any medication. As I did, I gently took authority over the spirit behind her symptoms and invited the Holy Spirit into her being. She initially looked dazed, as if a spirit had left her, and when I asked her how she felt, she said her symptoms were no more. Since she was feeling good, she didn't require any medication.

On one occasion, after returning from South Sudan, I came down with fever and rigors, and ended up overnight in the infectious disease unit at a London hospital. It turned out that I had malaria parasites in my blood, and hence received the appropriate treatment. God can heal anything and anyone, and also heals through research-based medicines.

Every Fruit has a Root

Jesus said: *'Make a tree good and its fruit will be good, or make a tree bad and its fruit will be bad, for a tree is recognized by its fruit. For out of the overflow of the heart the mouth speaks. The good man brings good things out of the good stored within him, and the evil man brings evil things out of the evil stored up in him. But I tell you that men will have to give an account on the Day of Judgment for every careless word they have spoken,'* (Matthew 12:33-36).

Some plants keep on flowering after the flowers are beheaded. They will only stop flowering once the roots are uprooted. Likewise, people may keep struggling with the same issue or symptom simply because they haven't dealt with the root. Until the root is addressed, the fruit will keep manifesting.

For example, if someone struggles with outbursts of anger, or panic attacks, then they may continue to have outbursts until the emotional root is healed. We can ask the Holy Spirit, *'Where is the root?'* or *'When did the symptoms first start?* The Holy Spirit may reveal a trauma or painful memory, and when this is healed the outbursts stop.

Some may ask, can the symptoms return if the root has been dealt with? Yes, especially if we allow another seed to grow. If I have forgiven someone, I may need to forgive them again and again, so I do not allow any seed of bitter-root-judgement to grow in my heart. Hence, Jesus told Peter to forgive not just seven times but seventy seven times. In other words, it is ongoing (Matthew 18:21). The enemy is prowling around sowing venomous seeds into the minds and hearts of God's people. Hence, just as we need to constantly de-weed our natural gardens, so we need to keep cleansing our hearts and minds from any unclean or negative thoughts we may have allowed in.

Spiritual Malaria

Whilst serving in Africa, I was asked to see a woman with malaria-like symptoms. Her blood was taken on two separate days and tested negative for malaria parasites both times. In case this was a false negative, (a false negative is when there are malaria parasites but they are not detected on testing), she decided to take some anti-malarial treatment. However, she didn't respond to two different anti-malarial drugs, so I offered to pray for her. At the time I offered to pray, I wasn't feeling particularly compassionate in my heart but rather tired and wanted to get home. As I prayed, her symptoms got worse and she told me to stop praying. This was because her symptoms were of spiritual origin that reacted to prayer. This was the reason she hadn't responded to the malaria drugs.

The interesting thing was about an hour later, I started to have the exact symptoms as she did. I developed a headache, nausea, felt very weak, feverish and dizzy. This had never happened to me before. I then wondered if the spirit in her had been transferred to me? I had read about this but never experienced it before. Just to be sure I didn't have malaria, I got myself tested, and sure enough it was negative. I felt a peace in my spirit that this was a true negative rather than a false negative. When I sought God, He told me to come into His presence and worship Him. As I did, I repented of my negative attitude and commanded the spirit behind my symptoms to leave. I was ninety percent better an hour later and was completely well by the next morning. What a lesson for me! I had malaria symptoms which tested negative, identical to the woman's symptoms, and occurred as a result of spiritual transference due to an open door in my heart to the enemy.

I called this 'spiritual malaria' and realized the enemy can counterfeit any sickness or disease. Satan can mimic anything for he is the father of lies (John 8:44). He may convince us we have real symptoms requiring medical attention, when we may require prayer ministry instead. I believe that the possible explanation for many physical illnesses which repeatedly test negative on investigation, causing confusion to medical staff, may be due to a spirit of infirmity behind the sickness which is counterfeiting the symptoms. It was a huge lesson when I realized Satan could counterfeit *any* sickness and disease.

Many times as a children's doctor I would come across cases where the real problem was the child's emotional or spiritual needs not being met. Usually when a person's symptoms don't fit a diagnosis or something doesn't sound quite right, then there is a strong possibility there is a spiritual or emotional root lurking somewhere in the background. Here, wisdom and discernment are required in such cases, along with the counsel of the Holy Spirit.

Spiritual & Emotional Roots

Here is a brief insight into some of the spiritual and emotional roots we may encounter, and are discussed in more detail in Volume Two.

Stress
Stress is a symptom not a diagnosis. Many take sick leave from work due to stress. The real question is what is causing the stress? It is known that stress and anxiety affect our body and health.

This is because emotional stress affects an important gland in the brain, known as the hypothalamus. The hypothalamus is responsible for the homeostasis of most organs in the body, such as the heart, bowel, lungs, immune system, nervous system, endocrine and urinary system. Hence, dis-eases and disorders come about when the hypothalamus is over stimulated by emotional stress.

Stress can precipitate stomach ulcers due to increased acid production, asthmatic problems from constriction of the airways, headaches or angina from hypertension, irritable or inflammatory bowel symptoms, skin problems (like eczema) and mental health issues. Basically, stress can affect or attack any part of our body. Stress related symptoms are like a wake-up call. We really need to deal with what's causing the stress instead of trying to treat the symptoms. Hence, medication for things like asthma, eczema, headaches, high blood pressure, acid-reflux, mental health issues and so on, do not necessarily cure but rather *suppress* the symptoms by dampening them down.

I don't believe God wants us to live a life filled with anxiety or stress. Anxiety and stress are linked to fear, and fear is linked to not feeling in control. We were created not to walk it alone, but with Him. We can choose to do things our own way or seek God's help and do it His way. His way is always the best, and it comes with peace and grace. To prevent disease and disorders occurring in the body, we need to deal with stress so the hypothalamus can normally function, keeping the body organs in homeostasis.

In the Message Bible we read: *'Walk with Me and work with Me - watch how I do it. Learn the unforced rhythms of grace. I won't lay anything heavy or ill-fitting on you'* (Mathew 11:29). God doesn't say that it will be easy if we follow Him and do His will, but He does say that He will give us His peace and grace, and be with us.

Unforgiveness

Many chronic body pains or physical illnesses may be the result of harbouring unforgiveness. I have witnessed many people receive physical healing, usually from some pain in their body, once they have chosen to forgive others, God or themselves.

The spirit of unforgiveness may cause chronic body pain, especially arthritic pain. I have seen people healed of pain in their shoulders, back, knees, hips, limbs, abdomen, neck and pelvis (basically anywhere in the body) when they have been willing to forgive *from their heart.*

Symptoms can return after being healed, especially if the person chooses to become resentful again. Unforgiveness is usually associated with an attitude of resentment, judgment, bitterness, hatred (to self or others), anger or jealousy. Dealing with these negative emotions is part of the healing process. Forgiveness from the heart not only frees us from these chains of negative emotions, but we can receive inner peace and freedom in exchange.

Unbelief

Jesus was unable to heal many in His hometown because of their lack of faith (Mathew 13:58, Mark 6:5-6). James says that the prayer offered in faith will make the sick person well (James 5:15). I believe we have to be careful not to tell someone they haven't been healed because of *their* lack of faith. Otherwise, we may be judging or pointing the accuser's finger at them. The faith of the person praying for the sick can release healing, as we see many times in the scriptures.

Healing is an act of God's grace, so we mustn't condemn people by saying it's their lack of faith or because of sin. God can still heal those with no faith or those who sin. However, we witness more healing when there is repentance of sin and a release of faith. People can have faith and not get healed, or have no faith and get healed. At times, God's healing is not as straightforward as we would like to think it is.

However, I think it is good practice to release faith in a person by asking them if they believe in God. And if so, do they believe He can heal them. Then as we pray, we can imagine (or see through the eyes of faith) the person with their body healed, and thank God for the healing. Let them test out the affected part of their body. Faith put in action releases healing.

False Beliefs

We all have false beliefs or distorted truths about our self, God or others, as a result of our negative experiences, skewed beliefs or what others have said. There are many things we have believed about ourselves or God that are simply not true, for they are not from God or not how He sees us. If we are not careful, these false beliefs may become a self-fulfilling prophecy. We may think, 'I will always have this condition. I will never get better'. Sure enough, this may happen because we have spoken these word-curses upon ourselves. The source of these false beliefs is Satan, who is the father of lies (John 8:44). Satan delights in telling us we are no good, will always suffer, or an illness is our identity and so on. He doesn't want us to know the truth about who God created us to be in Him, or discover God's will.

As we recognise each false belief or lie, and give it to Jesus, we can exchange it for His truth. Since Jesus is the Truth, He will always reveal His Truth to us whenever we ask. His truth can set our minds and hearts free.

Fears & Traumas

Fear can begin as a negative *emotion* but then develop into a *spirit* of fear. Fear is one of Satan's main strongholds. F.E.A.R means **False Evidence Appearing Real**. We make a fear as real as we choose to believe. '*For God did not give us a **spirit of fear** but a spirit of power, of love and of self-discipline*' (2 Timothy 1:7).

Jesus repeatedly said, 'Do not fear' to His disciples. There are many things we may fear, such as, fear of isolation, fear of man, fear of cancer, fear of death, fear of demons, fear of failure, fear of rejection, fear of heights, fear of doctors and the list goes on. Basically, we can fear anything. All fears are to be given to Jesus, and in exchange for each fear, we can receive His truth. '*I sought the Lord and He answered me; He delivered me from all my fears*' (Psalm 34:4).

Ongoing fear or anxious stress can lead to a compromised immune system. This is because fear and anxiety stimulate excess production of a steroid hormone called, *cortisol*. This is fine when we have short bursts of anxiety or fear, and the cortisol can return to normal. However, where there is ongoing fear and stress, there will be a chronic, sustained production of cortisol, and this will dampen or suppress the immune system. A compromised immune system makes someone at greater risk of developing sickness and disease.

Fears may be associated with traumas. In order to be free of the fear, the person will require healing of the traumatic event. This is usually done through the person encountering Jesus at the scene of the trauma. Examples of a traumatic event include abuse (verbal, emotional, physical or sexual), divorce, loss of a job, death of a loved one, or anything that causes significant emotional upset and stress in an individual's life. Symptoms that occur as a result of a trauma may be healed once the trauma has been addressed.

Rejection & Abandonment

Rejection and abandonment may produce the symptoms of anger, shyness, fear of man, isolation, loneliness, insignificance, self-hate, jealousy and so on. There are many things we may struggle with that are rooted in rejection or abandonment. Rejection may be passed down the bloodline, or occur at the moment of conception in an unwanted pregnancy.

We have all probably experienced some rejection in life, whether during childhood or adult life. People may or may not be aware of experiencing or perceiving rejection or abandonment. However, the Holy Spirit can reveal the areas of rejection or abandonment in our heart, and bring healing and acceptance through the powerful words of truth and love of our heavenly Father. We were created to be rooted and established in love (Ephesians 3:17).

Generational Sins & Curses

The Oxford English dictionary states a curse is: *'A solemn appeal to a supernatural power to inflict harm on someone or something'*. This may be to an individual or a group of people such as a family, village, a house, church or even a nation. Curses are more common than we think, and even Christians may curse one another by the negative words they speak (James 3:9).

A curse can come about through sin. When Cain killed Abel, God said his sinful act had now brought him under a curse (Genesis 4:11). God said if we obey His commands we will be blessed, but if we *disobey His commands then we will be cursed* (Deuteronomy 11:26). He then lists the sins that will bring curses when people choose to disobey and the blessings when people choose to obey God (Deuteronomy 27-28).

Many sicknesses or ongoing issues may be the result of generational sins. Some sins we may know and others we may not, but the Holy Spirit can bring to our attention the sins that need to be cleansed and set free from the bloodline. Generational sins usually come with a curse, and the curses can be broken once the sin has been addressed. There is no harm, only benefit, when we repent of the possible sins passed down the bloodline from our parents, grandparents and forefathers.

Jesus took all of our sins and all of our curses on the cross. He became our curse through His perfect sacrifice made for us. It is written: *'Anyone who is hung on a tree is under God's curse'* (Deuteronomy 21:23, Galatians 3:13). We no longer have to live under the power and effect of a curse, because by the blood of Jesus we can be set free from all curses. Hence, we can break a curse by the powerful Name of Jesus or through the powerful blood of Jesus.

Vows & Covenants

A vow or covenant is an oath or promise. Vows can be godly such as a wedding vow, or vows made to serve God. However, ungodly vows are made or spoken when a person is angry, hurt or thinking negative thoughts about themselves or others. We may say things like 'I will never...' or 'I will always...' In other cases, people may make covenants with satan or demonic spirits, when seeking demonic power or dedicating children to ancestral spirits. Ungodly vows and covenants should be broken, so an individual can receive inner freedom and healing from the harmful effects caused by them.

Unhealthy Relationships & Soul Ties

Healthy relationships are those where there is unconditional love and freewill, and this brings personal freedom and wholeness. However, an unhealthy relationship is bound by conditional love, fear, control, manipulation or abuse. Unhealthy soul-ties develop in unhealthy relationships. Soul-ties may be sexual or non-sexual. These are discussed in more detail in Volume two.

Healing the Broken-Hearted

Broken hearts may be come from lack of love as a result of rejection, abandonment or some form of abuse. Once the root has been identified, the area of pain or hurt in the heart can receive healing. The healing of a wounded area simply requires the love of God to bring complete restoration. This is explained in more detail in volumes two and three.

Witchcraft, Freemasonry and the Occult

The effects of witchcraft or involvement with the occult can bring sickness, disease and even death. There is no such thing as 'good' witchcraft such as white witchcraft. Any form of witchcraft is of demonic origin. Satan loves to deceive, because he is the father of lies. Many people go to 'faith healers', 'traditional healers', 'alternative therapists' or 'spirit masters' hoping they will get healed. The truth is most people who call themselves faith healers, alternative therapists, spirit masters or traditional healers, use a source of 'healing power' that is not from God. When we open ourselves up to the demonic realm, we are at risk of accidents, sicknesses or even premature deaths. Satan's mission is to kill, steal and destroy (John 10:10). Shortly after Saul went to visit a medium to enquire about the Philistine Army, he was killed in battle (1 Samuel 28:1-24). He had opened a door to the spirit of death after consulting a spiritualist.

'Let no-one be found among you who sacrifices his son or daughter in the fire, who practices divination or sorcery, interprets omens, engages in witchcraft, or casts spells, or who is a medium or spiritist or who consults the dead. Anyone who does these things is detestable to the Lord' (Deuteronomy 18:10-12). There are lists of occult activities that individuals or their ancestors may have taken part in at some point in life. By renouncing each activity, a person can be set free from demonic bondage. In Freemasonry, there are lists of demonic oaths and bondages that require renouncing for the individual to be free from the effects of these curses on their health. I have found that a general prayer usually isn't sufficient when it comes to dealing with freemasonry, since it involves a network of occult activity. However, there are specific prayers available that address the various degrees within freemasonry.[2]

Fetishes, Charms and 'Objects'

Before I stepped on the mission field, I was rather sceptical about objects having power. However, I have seen many people set free and healed when evil objects or fetishes were burnt and destroyed. Fetishes are the things witchdoctors give to heal a sick part of the body. They are pieces of string, usually with knots, and tied around the sick area of the body which may be the wrist, ankle, abdomen or neck. They usually carry demonic power. People have been instantly healed after fetishes have been removed and their power broken in Jesus' Name.

Likewise, charms and objects may carry evil power. We need to be careful of the gifts we receive from others. Objects may contain evil spirits that bring sickness and death. These include dragons, demon-looking objects, or things like crystals or charms that are meant to make you feel better. Also, weapons may carry evil spirits, depending on what they were used for. We can ask the Holy Spirit if there is anything we have that we may need to get rid of it, no matter how much we like it or who gave it to us.

Alternative Medicines and Therapies

I would like to add a note of caution here concerning alternative medicines and therapies used in modern day health care. We must be ever so careful not to open ourselves up to alternative medicines or therapies that are spiritually rooted in eastern religions or life energy forces. Though they may appear good and the people practicing them may be medical or Christians, we should first find out more about the source of power behind the healing.

As a Christian and a doctor, I believe we are either to seek Christ for our healing or go through the natural resources that God has provided, that science has researched and found beneficial to our health. I would be very careful of the alternative therapies that have no scientific proof for their healing powers. I have seen people delivered from spirits behind acupuncture, homeopathy, reflexology, reike and yoga. Deception is subtle when we seek healing from alternative sources, and this is where I believe we should first seek the counsel of the Lord.

'Many of those who believed now came and openly confessed their evil deeds. A number who had practiced sorcery brought their scrolls together and burned them publicly. When they calculated the value of the scrolls, the total came to fifty thousand drachmas. In this way the word of the Lord spread widely and grew in power' (Acts 19:18-19).

More is discussed about the spiritual influences of alternative medicines in Volume two.

This chapter gives insight into some of the possible roots behind a person's symptoms. The tools used for healing have been briefly highlighted and will be addressed in more detail in Volume two.

END NOTES

[1] Dr Wright, Henry W; *A More Excellent Way: Spiritual Roots of Disease Pathways to Wholeness*, Pleasant Valley Publications (2005)
[2] Stevens, Selwyn; *Unmasking Freemasonry, Removing the Hoodwink*, Jubilee Publishers.
[3] Kylstra, Chester: *Freemasonry in the family;* Restoring The Foundations.

9

Strongholds: Trees & Branches

Make a tree good and its fruit will be good, or make a tree bad and its fruit will be bad, for a tree is recognised by its fruit

Matthew 12:33

A spiritual garden can be viewed as the place in our hearts where we grow or develop Godly and ungodly spiritual fruit. The things we have spiritually nurtured in our hearts may range from the equivalent of young plants to mature trees. We can have godly plants in our spiritual gardens that produce good spiritual fruit and also ungodly plants that produce ungodly fruit, depending on what we have allowed to grow in our hearts over time. A stronghold can be compared to a tree with its roots and branches. If the roots are godly, then the fruit will be of the Spirit. However, if the roots are ungodly, then the fruit will be of the carnal or demonic nature. Hence, you know the root by its fruit (Matthew 7:16-20).

The things that imprison the spirit, soul and body can be known as *ungodly* or *demonic strongholds*. Strongholds usually refer to our ungodly behaviours, thoughts and attitudes. Christians, as well as non-Christians, have demonic strongholds. Jesus was the only one who had no demonic strongholds, for the enemy had no *hold* on Him. *'The prince of this world is coming.* **He has no hold on Me,***'* (John 14:30-31).

121

The Lord said to Cain: *'If you do not do what is right, sin is crouching at your door; it desires to have you but you must master it,'* (Genesis 4:7). Paul said something similar to the Ephesians: *'Do not let the sun go down while you are still angry, and do not give the devil a foothold,'* (Ephesians 4:27). Anger, along with other negative attitudes, opens the door of our hearts to the enemy and gives the enemy a foothold, until we address this particular issue by kicking the enemy out and closing the door (Ephesians 4:27). Let us look at strongholds in more depth.

What is a Stronghold?

A *natural stronghold* refers to a fortified place that offers protection against the enemy. Hence, a stronghold can be a place of refuge. In the Old Testament, there were strongholds on both the attacker's and the defender's side. They are referred to as mighty fortresses (Daniel 11:39) or a tower (Micah 4:8). David referred to his physical strongholds as places where he took refuge. *'Some Gadites defected to David, at his **stronghold** in the desert'* (1 Chronicles 12:8).

There are also the enemy's strongholds. *'In that day',* declares the Lord, *'I will destroy the cities of your land and tear down all your **strongholds'*** (Micah 5:11). Interestingly, the word stronghold (both singular and pleural) is mentioned around fifty times in the Old Testament but only once in the New Testament. In the Old Testament, it is referred to as a spiritual and a physical stronghold. Whereas, in the New Testament Paul refers to it as a spiritual stronghold: *'The weapons we fight with are not the weapons of the world. On the contrary, **they have divine power to demolish strongholds'*** (2 Corinthians 10:4). Here we see Paul is clearly referring to demonic strongholds.

Spiritual Strongholds

Just as we have natural, so we have spiritual strongholds. There are strongholds of God and strongholds of the enemy. The strongholds of God provide protection for us. David refers to God as being His stronghold: *'The Lord is the stronghold of my life- of whom shall I be afraid?'* (Psalm 27:1).

God's strongholds are our weapons. They are the very nature and character of God, also known as the fruit of the Spirit! Hence, they are His peace, love, forgiveness, joy, self-control, meekness, faith, truth, His Word, His power and authority.

So what are the enemy's strongholds? They are weapons the enemy uses to attack our minds. They are based on *lies, fears and pride.* Paul refers to them as 'arguments' and 'pretensions' that either exalt themselves above the knowledge of God or are not in agreement with His character: *'We demolish arguments and every pretension that sets itself up against the knowledge of God, and we take captive every thought, to make it obedient to Christ'* (2 Corinthians 10:4). Arguments may be seen as rebellious and prideful thoughts. Likewise, pretensions may refer to false beliefs and lies. These are attitudes and thoughts that do not come from the knowledge and character of God. Hence, we are to take authority over them and surrender them, as we choose to come under the Lordship of Jesus.

Ungodly strongholds are the very nature and character of Satan. They include pride, control, fear, doubt, lies, deception, lust, sexual sins, greed, power, selfish-ambition, intimidation, rejection, passivity, betrayal, victimization, selfishness, rebellion, religiosity, occult activity, anger, bitterness, unforgiveness, and so on. Hence, we must recognize these negative thought patterns and take authority over them by surrendering them to God, and exchanging them with the thoughts and attitude of Christ. This is like uprooting the ungodly roots and replacing it with a Godly seed from the fruit of the Spirit. This seed then needs to grow and be watered by the Spirit, as a person begins to take on the new mindset or attitude of Christ for each given situation.

Spiritual Blind Spots

In the natural, we all have what is known as a 'blind spot'. This is the area (or spot) in our right and left visual fields where there is no visual input. This is where the optic nerve has to pass through the optic disc. We are usually unaware of having this defect since the visual input from the rest of our optic field compensates. Just as we have natural blind spots we also have spiritual blind spots.

Being born-again and filled with the Holy Spirit doesn't make us exempt from having demonic strongholds. Usually the things that are holding us captive are the things we cannot see but others can see in us. These are our *spiritual blind spots*. It is much easier to see faults in someone else than it is in ourselves. This is why Jesus tells us to remove the plank from our own eyes before we move the speck from our brother's (Matthew 7:3-5).

I think for every critical or 'fault finding' thought we have against someone we probably have the same, if not more, faults ourselves. This is because we usually see in others the same issues we are struggling with. Hence that is why Jesus said we must first remove the planks from our own eyes.

Why do some people irritate us? It is probably because something in us has been triggered that we need to deal with. One challenging thing to do is to ask those who are close to us or know us well, what are our strong and weak points? Get ready to be surprised. When I dared to ask the question myself, I couldn't believe some of the remarks I received from those whom I love and had given permission to speak into my life. We need to pay attention, especially when more than one person is saying the same thing! Therefore, it is good to ask more than one person to speak the truth to us in love about ourselves.

On one occasion, I was feeling irritated by a fellow missionary, so I brought the issue to God. To my surprise, the Lord revealed that the reason I was feeling irritated, was because I had the same plank in my own eye. The issue I saw in her, I also had myself! The Lord convicted my heart to deal with my own issue first, then I would not respond so much when I saw the same thing in her. This was a huge lesson. So, when I get frustrated or worked up about anything, I simply ask God to shine His light on my own heart and deal with the area in my own heart first.

It is important to bring our spiritual blind spots into visibility so we can do something about them with the grace and help of the Holy Spirit. Most of the time we operate from our conscious level, but there is so much activity going on continually in our subconscious level. This is why we are usually unaware of the way we behave to others unless it is drawn to our attention. We need to be made aware of what is hidden in our subconscious level and this is where we need the help of the Holy Spirit to reveal any spiritual roots to ongoing issues in our lives.

Familial Strongholds

It is true to say that we are usually not aware of the ungodly strongholds we carry, especially when they are familiar to us. This may be because we have grown up with them or inherited them from our parents or the generations before them. We have become so familiar with them that we are unaware they are ungodly. They will prevent us from hearing God if they fill our minds with negative thoughts and ungodly spirits. These may be thoughts of self-pity, criticism, judgment, emotional manipulation, control, fear, pride, rejection, inadequacy, jealousy, lust, and so on. Hence, we need to be aware of them in order to deal with them. This is why we need each other and the Holy Spirit to show us our strongholds and how they manifest in our lives.

We can always ask God what our ungodly strongholds are. If we think we have none, then the first two that need addressing are the strongholds of pride and deception. Most of us will have been offended by someone or something at some point. We react to an offense with pride in our heart; *'How dare you say that about me,' 'Did you hear what they said? They said I was ...' 'Look what they have done...'* Our reaction is clearly one of pride. If we have no pride, then we will not get offended by what others say or do. Only Jesus was without sin, hence He had no demonic strongholds! The prince of this world had no *hold* on Him (John 14:30).

Trees & Branches

As already mentioned, each stronghold can be seen as a tree. The stronghold is like the main trunk or main issue we need to address. The fruit it produces are seen as the 'symptoms' or negative attitudes of our heart. The roots include the hidden or deep seated negative emotions, and will usually have an *access point*. The access point is when the seed for the stronghold first took root or gained access in our hearts and minds.

Some struggle with certain strongholds more than others, and this may be because the stronghold has come down the bloodline and been a part of a person's belief system and behavior from early on. Other strongholds may be rooted in a painful memory or traumatic event.

The stronghold of unforgiveness may have fruit or symptoms, such as, anger, resentment, bitterness, judgement, jealousy, hate and so on. The fruit is visible to others and noticed in a person's attitude and behaviour. Toxic fruit is produced from toxic roots. The roots are usually hidden, but the Holy Spirit who searches our innermost being, can shine His light on the roots. Unforgiveness may have the roots of rejection, orphan heart, self-hate or a victim mindset. If we want to stop producing the bad fruit, then we need to deal with the roots.

The Lord knows why we produce such fruit for He knows our past and sees the roots. With the help of the Holy Spirit, we can recognize and deal with the roots. Then we can replace it with the seeds that produce the fruit of His Spirit.

The Holy Spirit can bring to our attention the negative areas in our heart when dealing with strongholds. Someone may struggle to forgive a person if there are a cluster of roots that need removing. I found I could forgive someone only after I went through each thing they either did or didn't do that caused me grief or pain. When the last area was dealt with, it was as if the trunk could come out with ease. After that, I no longer felt any negative feelings or pain in my heart towards this person. If they walked in my room, I would feel fine to approach them.

Another stronghold may be a person struggling with pornography. The fruit may be lust, masturbation, false comfort, false power and perverse thoughts. However, the root may be one of rejection, abuse, lack of love, or perhaps someone introduced the person to pornography.

I met a person who struggled with the stronghold of fear. She would over-react with anxiety and fear in any given situation. It turned out that she had suffered with a few traumatic events in her childhood and also her mother was a very anxious and fearful person. Hence, there was a generational root and also roots from trauma in childhood. The healing was a process as each issue was addressed and her heart and mind were gradually being renewed with God's love and truth.

Each stronghold is based on our thoughts and attitudes, hence we need to replace these negative thoughts with Godly thoughts, as we experience and discover more about the character and mind of Christ.

Overcoming Strongholds

A plant or young shoot with shallow roots is easier to uproot compared to a tree with deep roots. The same applies to various strongholds we have allowed to grow in our 'spiritual garden'. The more we allow something ungodly to grow in our hearts, it will change from a young shoot or plant and become like a tree, as it develops into a stronghold. Major issues that we continually struggle with are more like trees or strongholds, and usually take a bit longer to uproot. Recognizing a stronghold is the start, but then choosing to live life in the opposite spirit is the daily challenge. One person may struggle with unforgiveness or anger, whereas another may struggle with pride. We all have issues, whether major or minor, and each of these needs uprooting from our spiritual gardens.

One way of overcoming strongholds is to apply something known as the five R's:
Recognize
Repent
Receive forgiveness
Renounce
Replace.

First, we need to recognize it is an issue, as the Holy Spirit reveals the unclean or ungodly areas in our heart. Second, we can repent as we choose to turn away from it and no longer come under it. Third, we can ask God to forgive us, and also forgive those who have passed the sin to us or in some way contributed to the sin. Once we have forgiven, then we can receive forgiveness for our negative thoughts or behavior, through the powerful blood of Jesus. This is not to be rushed but rather received in the heart. Fourth, we are now in a position to rebuke and renounce the spirit behind the stronghold, commanding it to leave, and not giving it a foothold anymore in our heart. And finally we can replace the stronghold with the heart and attitude of Christ, as we accept His truth and love in our hearts for this particular issue. This usually means choosing to go in the opposite spirit and attitude of heart, especially if the same thing happens again. Now, we can start to cultivate the fruit of the Spirit in our hearts, as we choose to respond with His Spirit in similar presenting situations.

Overcoming a stronghold requires perseverance, as the different branches and roots are dealt with one by one. For example, a controlling spirit may manifest in many ways, and each needs to be recognized and addressed in turn. Gradually the stronghold will weaken as each branch is addressed. It's as if we have to undo previous learnt behaviours or attitudes, as we rewire our minds with the attitude of Christ for each given situation. Each time we react in a negative manner, we need to ask the Lord how we should respond. He will give us His Kingdom perspective and attitude of heart for each situation. As we keep responding with the right attitude of heart, the stronghold becomes weaker until it has little or no more influence over us.

Another way of overcoming strongholds is to spend more time soaking in the presence of God. As we allow our hearts, minds and spirits to marinate in His presence, He can wash away any negative thoughts and renew our minds with His goodness and truth. As the Psalmist said, we become what we worship (Psalm 135:18). The longer we soak and abide in His presence, the more our minds and hearts become like Him. (For further reading on strongholds, I recommend *Restoring The Foundations*. [1] Also, see Appendix A for common groups of strongholds).

END NOTES

[1] Kylstra, Chester & Betsy: *Restoring The Foundations: An Integrated Approach to Healing Ministry:* (Proclaiming His Word, Aug 2001)

10

Compassion, Faith & Authority

*I have given you authority to trample on snakes and scorpions
and to overcome all the power of the enemy*

Luke 10:19

God can heal anyone through any way He chooses. However, over the years I have discovered three basic requirements for ministering healing: *compassion, faith* and *authority*. God gives us these as we step into the healing ministry, but each requires nurturing and further developing, through our personal intimate relationship with Him.

Compassion Releases Healing

A few months after I joined Iris Global in Mozambique, I had a vivid and prophetic dream. In the dream, I was 38-weeks pregnant and started going into labour. I thought how could this be possible unless it was an immaculate conception? Somewhat shocked, I yelled, 'Stop!' and halted the labour. As I woke up, I thought, *'What was that dream all about?'* After discussing it with fellow missionaries, I realized my dream represented a 'spiritual pregnancy' where I was due to give 'spiritual birth'. I had never heard of this before but those with me had experienced something similar. Just as we can give birth in the natural, so we can give birth to something that the Holy Spirit has sown in the supernatural. I have realized that spiritual births can apply to men as well as women, after credible men of God have testified to experiencing something similar.

Two weeks later (when I would have been 40 weeks pregnant), I felt something inside me had to come out. It felt strange and I didn't know what was going on until someone prayed with me. It felt like I was going into labour. Funnily enough, this was not new to the person who was praying with me. She commented how she had been a 'spiritual midwife' before. Tears flooded down my face as I felt a deep burden within my spirit. It felt like my spirit was groaning within and it came in waves, as if in labour. Paul said: *'We do not know what we ought to pray for, but the Spirit Himself intercedes for us with groans that words cannot express. And He who searches our hearts knows the mind of the Spirit, because the Spirit intercedes for the saints in accordance with God's will'* (Romans 8:26-27).

After forty minutes, it gradually came to a finish and I felt exhausted. I asked God, *'What was that all about? What had I given birth to spiritually?'* The answer was clear. It was His **compassion**! He said I needed His compassion, for it was through His compassion that His healing would flow to the people! The timing was perfect because we were about to start the mobile clinics for the bush outreaches. Jesus was moved with *compassion* when He saw the sick and suffering around Him. Through love and compassion, He healed them (Matthew 9:36, 14:14, 20:34, John 11:35).

Sometimes, whilst praying I would feel an overwhelming compassion for people, and could sense the power of the Holy Spirit minister healing. I somehow knew in my spirit that the person had been healed. However, on one occasion when I prayed for an old woman's chronic body pain, nothing happened. Then to my utter amazement, the Holy Spirit convicted me on the spot. He said, *'You didn't pray with compassion!'* My mind was elsewhere as I was praying for her, so I repented for not engaging my heart. Then when I prayed again with my heart, her pain went and she was healed. What a lesson on compassion and healing! The Holy Spirit was right on my case and I could not pray without His compassion. Jesus had compassion on all those He healed.

Compassion is a gift of God. It is more than sympathy. Sympathy is from our flesh, and a sense of feeling sorry for others but not necessary doing anything to help. Compassion is from the Spirit, and helps us to feel God's heart for His people. Compassion releases an incentive or passion to do something for a person. Compassion from God compels us to pray for others with His heart. It opens the door for His healing to flow.

The late Jill Austin (founder of Master Potter Ministries) gave this word from God: *'The key to apostolic authority is love. If people want to move in signs and wonders and miracles, if they want to see heaven breaking in to take whole territories, then they need to discover My heart and My compassion. Then I will give them the power to set the captives free and the anointing to see the sick healed and the dead raised.'* [1] We grow in compassion as we mature in sonship through our personal walk with God.

Faith Releases Healing

When Jesus prepared for the cross, He said something amazing: *'I tell you the truth, **anyone who has faith in Me** will do what I have been doing. He will do even greater things than, these because I am going to the Father,'* (John 14:12). Anyone who has FAITH will do what He did: heal the sick, set the captives free, cleanse the lepers, be transported in the Spirit, and raise the dead! And much more than this!

Faith was required to heal the sick. Either the faith of Jesus or His disciples, or the faith of a friend or family member, or the faith of the sick person, allowed healing to flow. Jesus told Jairus: *'Just believe!'* and his daughter would be healed (Luke 8:50). Jesus replied to the faith of the Centurion: *'Go! It will be done just as you believed it would'*, and his servant was healed at that very hour (Mathew 8:13). Jesus said to the woman who touched His garment that *her faith* had healed her (Mathew 9:22, 14:36). He said to the blind man that *according to his faith* he would be healed (Mathew 9:27-30). Jesus healed only a few in His hometown because of the *lack of faith* (Mark 6:5-6). The disciples asked Jesus why they failed to heal the fitting boy, and Jesus said it was due to their lack of faith (Mathew 17:20). When Jesus approached the demon-possessed man on the other side of the lake, it was through Jesus'

131

faith and authority that the demons responded to His command (Mark 5:1-17).

It is good to be with people of faith when praying for the sick and kindly ask those who are not of such faith to leave or wait outside. Even Jesus had to remove or ask to leave, those who carried doubt or had a spirit of mockery. When He went to Jairus' daughter, He only took Peter, James and John inside along with Jairus and his wife. He put everyone else outside (Mark 5:40). Likewise, when Jesus prayed for the blind man at Bethsaida, He took the blind man *and led him outside the village* and told him not to go back into that village (Mark 8:22-26).

An old African woman crawled into my clinic, full of pain and swelling in her bowed legs. At first I struggled to believe she could be healed for her pain was so severe. So I closed my eyes in prayer, and imagined her legs upright and standing before the Lord in worship and praise. As I spoke these words and commanded her legs to dance before the Lord, I took hold of her hand and lifted her up. Her face expressed such pain as I pulled her forth. I continued to pray and thank God for His healing power. Her expression started to change. The intense pain gradually left her face as she started to smile. Not only did the pain go, but she was able to dance on the spot, thanking God as she did. Though her legs remained bowed, she was healed and free of pain.

I was in a Muslim village when a blind lady came to the clinic for treatment. She had to feel her way into the medical tent, with her daughter guiding her in front. She became suddenly blind two years ago and now her eyes had developed a white glaze. At first I told her I had nothing to offer and she needed to see an eye doctor. However, there was no eye doctor in her African town. So we offered to pray for her. Our eyes were on Jesus as we asked Him to heal her. We broke off witchcraft and curses, and commanded any spirit behind her symptoms to leave. She started to see light, though the colours were only black and white. We prayed again, and she could now see colours but little else. We prayed again and now she saw moving objects like tree trunks (sounds familiar??). We prayed a fourth and final time and now she saw everyone in the tent. She described accurately what I was wearing and saw my glasses and stethoscope. This was the result of having the faith of a mustard seed (Luke 17:6). When healing begins, even if the person only feels slightly better, we shouldn't give up but continue in faith, until full healing has occurred.

Another word for faith is 'RISK'. The Lord revealed this to me when I was out at sea on a catamaran. As I ventured out with the boatman, the winds started to get up and we went hurtling along at full speed. The ride was both exhilarating and scary, for it felt like we were going to capsize each time the catamaran submerged its side in the sea. When we got back to shore, I thought, 'Wow, that was absolutely amazing!' I encouraged a friend to have the same experience and go on the catamaran, but she fervently said 'No way!' She wasn't going to take the risk. She decided to stay on the shore where she felt in control, secure and safe. This is when the Lord clearly revealed to my spirit that faith is 'risk taking'. Radical faith is like stepping out the boat to walk on water. Some may say, *'Yes, but what if it doesn't happen? What if...?'* Faith requires obedience to the promptings of the Spirit. The Lord has given us two legs: one is faith and the other is obedience. To step out in faith requires us to step out in obedience to God's will. Though it may initially seem daunting as we step out in faith to ride the waves with God, in return we will have such an amazing experience beyond what we can dream or imagine.

Faith is a willingness to step into the unknown, along unchartered territory, when God asks us to follow Him. James challenged all believers to *act* with faith, for faith without actions is dead. *'Faith by itself, if it is not accompanied by action is dead. But someone will say, "You have faith; I have deeds". Show me your faith without deeds, and I will show you my faith by what I do'* (James 2:14-26). Jesus invites us to walk on water with Him. This is radical faith - stepping out into the unknown in obedience to God's will. Our flesh tells us, 'don't be stupid...you will sink', but our spirit hears the Lord inviting us to live a life of radical faith and obedience.

Faith is seeing things through our spiritual eyes, before we see it happen in the natural. God gives us faith to declare what we see in the Spirit, so it will take place on earth. Hence Jesus taught us to pray: *'Your Kingdom come, Your will be done, on earth as it is in heaven'*. Faith is being sure of what we hope for and certain of what we do not see (Hebrews 11:1). Jesus is looking for people who live by faith (2 Corinthians 5:7, Luke 18:8).

One day, as I was meditating on faith, I saw the letters F.A.I.T.H and the following immediately came to mind:

F- Fear the Lord.
The fear of the Lord is in the hearts of those who live by faith. Those who fear the Lord, choose to fear Him instead of the enemy. Ungodly fear quenches faith. However, the awesome, reverential fear of the Lord causes us to step out in faith and obey Him. Abraham was a man of faith who feared the Lord. All the great men and women of faith, both revered and obeyed the Lord (Exodus 14:31).

A- Action
Faith requires action, because faith without action is dead (James 2:26). Faith requires us to do what the Lord has asked us to do. Radical faith involves stepping out of the boat and walking on water. To do this, we must keep our eyes on Jesus and not our peripheral circumstances.

I- Identity
Men and women of faith know their spiritual identity with God. They know who they are, because they have an intimate relationship with Him. Since they personally know Him in their hearts, they respond by faith when He speaks. Those who struggle with their spiritual identity, also struggle with their faith. Our faith increases the further we mature as His sons and daughters.

T- Trust Him
Faith is trusting in God and in His word and promises. It is trusting that He is with us and is faithful to do what He has promised. Trust also means surrender. We respond in faith by surrendering our will and plans to Him. Hence, trust in the Lord with all your heart and lean not on your own understanding (Proverbs 3:5).

H- Hearing

Faith increases when we open our hearts to hear God, and respond to His word and Spirit. Faith comes from hearing and hearing comes from the word of God (Romans 10:17). Fear listens to the enemy, but faith listens to God.

Authority Releases Healing

Compassion, faith and spiritual authority release healing. Prayer is not necessarily the number of words we say, or the volume we shout, but the authority we carry. Jesus didn't pray long prayers when He healed the sick. He actually spoke directly to the sickness or demon(s) with few words. He *'rebuked the fever'* and it left (Luke 4:39). He commanded the demon to *'Be quiet!'* then *'Get out!'* (Mark 1:25). To the demon-possessed, He drove out the evil spirits with just *a word* (Mathew 8:17). To the leper, He commanded, *'Be clean!'* (Mark 1:41). When raising Lazarus from the dead, He spoke with authority: *'Lazarus, come forth!'* (John 11:43). To the man born blind, He commanded him to: *'Go, wash in the pool of Siloam!'* and as he did, he was healed (John 9:7). When He was asked to heal a man who was both deaf and mute, He commanded his ears and mouth: *'Be opened!'* (Mark 7:34).

When evil spirits encountered Jesus, they bowed down before Him, because they knew the authority He carried. *'For He had healed many, so that those with diseases were pushing forward to touch Him. Whenever the **evil spirits saw Him, they fell down before Him and cried out, "You are the Son of God".** But He gave them strict orders not to tell who He was'* (Mark 3:10-12). Likewise, when the man who was demon possessed with thousands of demons saw Jesus from a distance, he ran, fell on his knees, and the demons shouted: *'What do You want with me, Jesus, Son of the Most High God?'* (Mark 5:6). All demons fear Jesus because they know who He is and the authority He carries. Hence, *'Every knee will bow in Heaven, on earth and under the earth and every tongue confess that Jesus Christ is Lord'* (Philippians 2:10-11). Amen.

We need to be aware of the authority we carry as sons and daughters of the King, and the areas where He has called us to minister. There are low and high-ranking demons (or demonic powers) in the spiritual realm, as well as principalities that rule

135

over regions or nations (Ephesians 6:12). There are different ways to deal with high-ranking demons, and this is not for the beginner but for those who know their level of authority given to them by God. Even angelic beings don't rebuke Satan, but say: '*The Lord rebuke you*' (Jude 9, Zech 3:2). Likewise, when dealing with high-ranking demons, it is wise not to approach them directly, but to address each situation or 'case' by taking it to the Courts of Heaven. Here we present each issue to God our Judge and Jesus our Advocate, asking for justice, forgiveness, healing and freedom. (More on 'Approaching the Courts of Heaven' is discussed in volume 3.)

When Jesus commissioned His disciples, He said: '*All authority in Heaven and on earth has been given to Me. Therefore, go and make disciples of all nations, baptizing them in the Name of the Father, Son and Holy Spirit and teaching them to obey everything that I have commanded you*' (Matthew 28:18).

Kingdom Authority

Kingdom authority is the authority given by God to those who have a personal relationship with Him. *So when does a person have Kingdom authority?* A person has authority the moment they accept Jesus into their heart to be their Lord and Saviour. Many Spirit-filled believers witness healings and miracles as they start praying for others in the Name of Jesus. I have seen little children who personally know Jesus, have authority to heal the sick. They lay hands on them and say a simple prayer like 'be healed in Jesus Name' or 'sickness go, in Jesus Name' and the person starts to recover. God rejoices when His little ones learn to walk in His authority. Many may think pastors are the only ones who have authority when in actuality the Lord gives authority to all His Spirit-filled believers. One of the roles of a pastor is to encourage and empower the body of believers to walk in their inherited authority as children of the King.

I was with a group of small children teaching on healing when one little boy bravely shared that he had been having nightmares. Another child in the group had also suffered with nightmares but after receiving prayer was healed and didn't have them anymore. So I asked the child who was healed to pray for this little boy. The next week when we met again, the little boy testified to having no more nightmares. Praise God that out of the mouths of little ones He has ordained praise and given them authority to overcome the enemy! (Psalm 8:2).

Kingdom authority is not gained from going to Bible school or from studying theology or on a basis of who you know. Rather, it comes from an intimate relationship with God. Jesus never went to Bible College and didn't take a theology degree. Instead, He learnt directly from His Father and through the scriptures. *'When Jesus had finished saying these things, the crowds were amazed at His teaching, because* **He taught as one who had authority,** *and not as their teachers of the law'* (Matthew 7:28-29). *'Then He went down to Capernaum, and on the Sabbath began to teach the people. They were amazed at His teaching, because* **His message had authority***'* (Luke 4:32).

The disciples were seen as unschooled and ordinary people (Acts 4:13). Yet they walked in power and authority being under the authority of Jesus. *'When the seventy-two disciples returned to Jesus they said, "Lord, even the demons submit to us in Your Name", and Jesus replied, "I saw Satan fall like lightning from Heaven. I have* **given you authority to trample on snakes and scorpions and to overcome all the power of the enemy;** *nothing will harm you"'* (Luke 10:17-19). Jesus has given us authority to overcome ALL the power of the enemy.

Satan has power but no authority for he was kicked out of God's Kingdom as a result of rebellion, pride and selfish-ambition. He only has the power of a fallen cherub angel. However, when Adam and Eve sinned, they gave their authority to him. When Satan tempted Jesus, he showed Him the kingdoms of the world and said: *'I will give you all their authority and splendour,* **for it has been given to me***, and I can give it to anyone I want to'* (Luke 4:6). Therefore, he only has authority that has been given to him by man.

After Jesus took all our sin on the cross, He went down to Hades and took back the keys that Satan had stolen (Revelation 1:18). Keys represent authority. Jesus took back the stolen authority. When He appeared to His disciples, He said: *'**All authority in Heaven and on earth has been given to Me. Therefore, go and make disciples....***' (Matthew 28:18). If Jesus has *all* authority, this means Satan now has *none!*

137

It is important we know there are different levels of authority in the Kingdom of God. The moment we are born-again of the Spirit, we have some level of spiritual authority. However, we *grow* in authority from intimacy with God. The greater the depth of intimacy, through the yielding of our hearts to God, the greater is the authority.

Isaiah refers to the 'governmental' authority that rested on the shoulders of the Messiah (Isaiah 9:6). This is authority which comes with responsibility, since it rests upon those who are called to govern God's people. Hence governmental authority rests on the apostles, prophets, evangelists, pastors and teachers, whose purpose is to train and equip the body of Christ (Ephesians 4:11).

The Greek word for church is *Ekklesia*. When Jesus said to Simon Peter, *'On this rock I will build My Ekklesia,'* He was referring to a legislative assembly or a people who would carry governmental authority to rule the nation (Matthew 16:18). God is the one who appoints us to positions of governmental authority, not man. This is because He is the one to release such authority for the work in His Kingdom. The people God appoints have walked with Him through seasons of brokenness and humility, having overcome many tests and trials in their spiritual journey and growth. The tests are not on paper, but rather tests of the heart. We notice this in the lives of people like Joseph, Moses, David, Esther and Paul, as well as modern day anointed leaders.

Growing in Authority

The degree we grow in authority is influenced by *humility, obedience, surrender, a servant heart, spiritual identity, prayer and fasting,* and *overcoming the works of the enemy.* Let us look at these in more detail.

Humility

King Jesus demonstrated what it meant to have a humble servant heart: *'Who being in the very nature God, didn't consider equality with God something to be grasped, but made Himself nothing, taking the very nature of a servant, being made in human likeness. And being found in appearance as a man, He humbled Himself and became obedient to death- even death on a cross. Therefore God exalted Him to the highest place and gave Him the Name that is above every name, that at the Name of*

Jesus, every knee should bow, in Heaven and on earth and under the earth and confess that Jesus Christ is Lord' (Philippians 2:6-7). God promoted Jesus to the highest place of authority in His Kingdom because of His humility and obedience unto death.

Jesus demonstrated complete submission to His Father's will and authority, but also submitted to the government authorities. He said: *'Whoever humbles himself like a little child is the greatest in the Kingdom of Heaven'* (Mathew 18:4). Those who carry significant authority in His Kingdom are those who walk in great humility. One of the things I noted in the vision of the H.M.S ship, was that the senior officials who carried significant authority exuded immense humility.

Jesus gives His grace to the humble. His grace is the supernatural power and ability to do what we can't do in the natural. We become more aware of His grace the further we mature in our relationship with God. Jesus was full of grace. He learnt how to depend on His Father for everything. Nothing He did was in His own strength or flesh. Everything He did was through the power of the Spirit. The Lord increases His authority in those who choose to live by grace.

Obedience

Jesus was obedient, even unto death on the cross. Whatever His Father asked, He did. He obeyed His Father's will, whatever the cost. Through His obedience unto death, God gave Him the Name above all names that at the Name of Jesus every knee will bow and confess Him as Lord. Obedience means doing whatever God asks, even when we don't want to. Obedience to His will releases the necessary authority for the work He has called us to do.

Surrender

In order to receive authority, we need to know how to come under authority. A submissive heart is vital in God's Kingdom. Each time we fail to surrender our hearts to God we fall in areas such as; self-ambition, pride, rebellion, stubbornness, self-opinion, self-focus or building our own empires. Surrender means laying down everything and giving up our rights to God. This includes the right to marriage, right to be wealthy, right to be successful, right to have a career or status and so on. A fully surrendered life includes laying down our desires and plans, our opinions, our likes and dislikes, our judgments and our flesh. It is laying down our 'self,' until we reach the point where 'I no longer live but Christ lives in me' (Galatians 2:20). Jesus called us to follow Him, and this includes the way of the cross. A fully surrendered life is a sacrificial life, where we no longer live for self, but for Him who sacrificed His life for us. As we lay down each area of our carnal nature, we are allowing an increase in capacity for His Spirit in us. The less of our flesh means the more of His Spirit.

Servant Heart

Jesus demonstrated a servant's heart as He took up a towel and washed His disciple's feet. He told Peter that unless he let Him wash his feet, he would have no part in Him (John 13:7-8). He wanted to make it clear that He came to serve and not be served. We are to do likewise. Pride, control and rebellion led Satan to lose his Kingdom authority. We need to let God deal with these areas in our hearts, otherwise they will hinder our growth in sonship and authority. Jesus carried the heart of a yielded servant. Hence, if we want to lead *with* spiritual authority, we need to be able to serve *under* authority. A servant heart is an essential requirement. As Bill Johnson once said, 'We are to rule with the heart of a servant and serve with the heart of a king'. This means, we use our God given authority to serve and empower others, being aware of the unlimited resources we can access from the King.

Prayer & Fasting

Fasting releases spiritual authority. When we fast, we are submitting our flesh to our spirit, as we abstain from food or other things. Our spirit grows in authority when we yield our flesh to God and let Him be Lord in our life. Fasting should play a part in our life. We sanctify our bodies, soul and spirit through prayer and fasting, and this influences the level of authority we carry. I have not yet seen a man or woman of God who carries significant kingdom authority and doesn't fast. Fasting has become a part of their lifestyle.

The Lord may call us to fast during specific seasons, especially where there is need for breakthrough. As we fast, shifts will take place in the spiritual realm, and our spirit will become more sensitive to the prompting of the Holy Spirit. (See chapter 12, *'When we Fast'*).

Spiritual Identity

We grow in authority as we mature in our spiritual identity. A little child may not be aware of their own identity until they start to mature as a son or daughter. As they mature as God's royal sons and daughters, they will become aware of the increase in their authority.

Authority goes hand-in-hand with developing in our spiritual identity. This requires a revelation in our heart. Those who walk in Kingdom authority have a deep awareness of who they are in Christ. This is the result of walking intimately with Him and living in His presence. As we take on our royal identity, we learn to carry His power and authority, by walking in His grace and humility. The mighty warriors of God are those who walk in humility with an awareness of their identity as royal sons and daughters of the King.

Ability to Overcome

Once we have overcome an enemy stronghold, we are in a position to help others overcome. This is because it no longer has a hold on us. It is like climbing up a mountain. Once we have mastered how to get to the next level, we are in a position to help others reach that same level. Hence, whatever we have overcome, we now have the authority to help others overcome.

David, Moses, Joseph and the Apostles, all had mountains to climb and obstacles to overcome before they entered their callings and destinies. When Jesus was tested, He overcame with humility, surrender and obedience to God's will. After overcoming each trial and battle, God gave Him governmental authority to fulfill His mission on earth. Jesus said: *'**To him who overcomes and does My will to the end, I will give authority over the nations**, just as I have received authority from My Father'* (Revelation 2:26).

What Do We Have Authority Over?

Naturally, we are aware of the authority we carry in our workplace, family or home. Likewise, we need to be aware of the authority we carry as God's children in His Kingdom. It is important to know the boundaries for the designated level of authority we carry, especially when praying over regions or dealing with principalities. Sometimes, it may not be right to pray for someone but instead to refer to someone else.

Authority Over Demons

Spirit-filled believers have power and authority to overcome the works of the enemy. Jesus gave us authority to heal the sick, cleanse the leper, raise the dead and set the captives free. Demons have to surrender to the Name of Jesus, because at His Name every knee shall bow (Philippians 2:10). However, demons only respond to those who carry spiritual authority. When the seven sons of Sceva went around saying: '*In the Name of Jesus, whom Paul preaches, I command you to come out...*' they were challenged when a demonic spirit replied, '*Jesus I know, and Paul I know, but who are you?*' (Acts 19:13-17). There is power in the Name of Jesus for those who walk in His authority.

When Jesus released His authority and power to the disciples, it was to bring salvation, healing and deliverance to the people. When they returned from healing the sick and casting out demons, Jesus said: '*I have given you authority to trample on snakes and scorpions and to **overcome all the power of the enemy**; nothing will harm you*' (Luke 10:19).

Jesus said to Peter: '*I will give you the keys of the Kingdom of Heaven; whatever you bind on earth will be bound in Heaven and whatever you loosen on earth will be loosened in Heaven*' (Matthew 16:19). Some may argue that these words were for Peter, but Jesus spoke the same words again a few chapters later, to a much wider audience. '*I tell you the truth, whatever you bind on earth will be bound in heaven, and whatever you loose on earth will be loosed in heaven. Again, I tell you that if two of you on earth agree about anything you ask for, it will be done for you*' (Matthew 18:18-20). When we agree on something as we pray together in the Spirit, God will release His power, authority, along with His ministering angels (Hebrews 1:14).

The keys represent spiritual authority. We can take authority over our situations or circumstances, especially when things are going wrong or coming against us. To loosen is to release or set free. To bind is to tie up. Jesus specifically referred to us binding the strongman or demonic spirits in one another: *'If I drive out demons by the Spirit of God, then the Kingdom of God has come. Or again, how can anyone enter a strongman's house and carry off his possessions unless he first ties up the strongman?'* (Mathew 12:29). First, we are to tie up or bind the demonic stronghold (evil spirit), then we can cast it out and loosen the person or ourselves from being under its influence.

I believe we have authority in Christ to free each other, as well as ourselves, from demonic spirits. This includes taking authority over sickness and anything we find personally attacking us or coming in the midst of relationships.

However, there may be cases where we don't have the level of authority required to tackle a certain sickness or issue. This requires discernment, knowing when to refer to others who have more experience and authority in this area. If the Lord wants us to take on such cases, then He will guide and equip us, as He releases His strategy for each case. In some cases, we may feel led to fast, or perhaps to take the situation to the Courts of Heaven, especially when dealing with high-ranking demonic powers, or when requiring significant breakthrough. Sometimes, healing is a process, as God deals with each of the areas in our heart.

Authority Over Our Bodies

We all have authority over our bodies, because there is power in our tongue. We have the power to curse or bless with the words we speak (James 3:9-10). There is a saying: *'You are what you eat'.* Likewise, we are what we think or speak. If we speak curses over ourselves, then we can be effected by what we say. And if we speak blessings over ourselves, then we can be blessed. We must learn not to speak negative comments to our bodies but instead thank God for creating us in His image. If there is anything that is malfunctioning, then we can command it to function properly in Jesus' Name and keep blessing it until it functions normally again.

One lady with high blood pressure decided to bless her blood pressure and commanded it to be normal. It gradually returned to normal, hence she didn't require medication.

Many times people have asked me to pray for their symptoms but if they are Spirit-filled believers, I have encouraged them to take authority over their bodies themselves. There was a lady who had been struggling to eat food. Anything she ate caused her to experience upper abdominal pain. The excess acid she produced caused her intense stomach pain and now she had a fear of eating. First, she repented and renounced the fear of eating. Then she took authority over her acid production. She commanded her stomach to produce the right amount needed to digest her food and declared 'peace' to her stomach. She then blessed her stomach and thanked God for creating it. I was with her when she next had a meal and she ate without experiencing any stomach pain. She was amazed. I encouraged her to walk in authority instead of fear, and she could eat any food with no further symptoms.

We mustn't accept negative comments or medical labels on our bodies or speak negatively about them but instead take authority over our organs or body parts, and command them to function normally, as God designed them to do, in the Name of Jesus. When we thank God for our bodies and speak blessings on them instead of curses, it is powerful.

When Paul was shipwrecked on the island of Malta, a snake wrapped itself around his arm but he threw it off. Everyone thought he would die of poisoning but he didn't. He had authority to overcome any harmful effects the snake had onhim(Acts28:5).

Similarly, Jesus was never sick, for the enemy was never allowed to have a hold on Him. Likewise, we shouldn't allow the enemy to have a hold on us. The cells in our bodies respond to our authority. Hence, we can command our cells to function normally and command the sickness, pain or cancer cells to go in Jesus' Name.

There was an old lady I saw on an island in Mozambique who had recently accepted Jesus into her heart. However, soon after this, she started to have 'fits'. There was much witchcraft on the island, hence, the fits were likely to be spiritual in nature as a result of her becoming a new believer in Christ. I told her to take authority over her body and command the fits to go in Jesus' Name. An hour or so later, when she felt a fit coming on, she took authority over it and it instantly stopped. Since then she has had no more fits.

There have been times when I have felt pain or numbness in various parts of my body, and instantly commanded it to go and it has left within minutes. However, there have been times when I have struggled to shake off symptoms and may have required medication. Even if this were to happen, it is good practice to take authority over our symptoms and keep cleansing our bodies with the precious blood of Jesus. Communion is a powerful medicine because many have received healing through regularly taking Communion (See the chapters *Blessing your Body* and *Power in the Blood* in Volume two).

Compassion, faith and authority, are important gifts and also fruit of the Spirit for releasing healing and freedom. They are like spiritual muscles: the more they are exercised, the stronger they become and greater is the fruit and spiritual reward.

END NOTES

[1] Austin, Jill; *Dancing With Destiny; p94 (Chosen, 2007)*

11

Blockages To Healing

*The knowledge of the secrets of the Kingdom of Heaven
has been given to you*

Matthew 13:11

There may be different reasons why people aren't healed and the more we understand the scriptures and nature of God, the more we will understand the possible blockages to healing. Even Paul was unable to heal his friend Trophimus, whom he had to leave behind in Miletus (2 Timothy 4:20).

Some of the blockages may be due to us not addressing the underlying spiritual or emotional roots. Sometimes, the Lord may allow the righteous to die to be spared from evil: *'The righteous perish, and no-one ponders it in his heart; devout men are taken away and no-one understands that the righteous are taken away to be spared from evil,'* (Isaiah 57:1).

There will be times when we just don't know why someone wasn't healed or died from an illness. Likewise, there will be times where the testimonies given by those who have been healed may expose the underlying roots or blockages to the healing.

147

Reasons for Blockages to Healing

Here are some possible reasons for the blockages to healing.

Unbelief

One of the major hindrances to healing is not having the faith to believe God can heal. Some may have lost faith through disappointment. When the disciples asked Jesus why they couldn't drive out the demon from the fitting boy, He replied it was because of their lack of faith (Matthew 17:20, Luke 9:41). The father of the fitting boy asked Jesus to heal his son *if He can*. Jesus replied: '*If you can? Everything is possible to him who believes,*' at which the father replied: '*I do believe, help me overcome my unbelief,*' (Mark 9:23-24). A few chapters later Jesus said: '*Have faith in God. Truly I say to you, whoever says to this mountain "Be taken up and cast into the sea" and does not doubt in his heart, but believes that what he says is going to happen, it will be granted to him. Therefore I say to you, all things for which you pray and ask, believe that you have received them, and they will be granted you,*' (Mark 11:22-24, Math 21:21).

James, one of the half-brothers of Jesus, said the prayer offered in *faith* will make the sick person well (James 5:15). Jesus commented He was unable to heal many in His home town because of their lack of faith (Math 13:58, Mark 6:5-6). However, when the woman who had been suffering with a chronic bleed, reached out and touched His garment, He said: '*Daughter your faith has healed you. Go in peace,*' (Luke 8:43-48).

When I have struggled to believe God could heal a particular person, I have closed my eyes and imagined the person healed. Paul prayed: '*I pray that the light of God will illuminate the eyes of your imagination,*' (Ephesians 1:18). We need to imagine with our eyes and believe with a heart of faith that healing is possible. If healing doesn't happen the first time, we can try again and again, and not give up!

The Lord made it possible for us to minister healing to people of other faiths, on a few of the islands off the coast of Mozambique. He revealed to my spirit how He wanted to heal the people so they could experience His love and power. As I responded in faith, I felt inspired to ask each person if they believed in God. Their answer would be 'yes'. Next, I would ask if they believed God could heal them. Even though they had never witness a healing, they each thought 'yes, or why not?' Simply by opening up their hearts to God with faith, most received healing and their symptoms improved.

False Belief

Whereas unbelief is belief that God hasn't the power or ability to heal a person, false belief is when we believe God *doesn't want* to heal someone. Some people believe they are to remain ill and God doesn't want to heal them. Jesus healed all who came to Him. Sickness and disease are not from God. It is not His will and plan for us to suffer sickness, though He may use it for His glory. God was able to display His glory through the man born blind (John 9:3). God said: '*I am the Lord who heals you,*' (Exodus 15:26). A woman who had been crippled for eighteen years as a result of demonic bondage, was instantly healed and set free by Jesus (Luke 13:16). She came to Him and He healed her.

Sometimes, the timing may not be right. This sounds controversial, but the Lord may give prophetic words or knowledge when He is going to heal someone. It is not that the Lord won't or can't heal, but that sometimes we need various layers removing before we are fully healed. It is a bit like Lazarus having to remove his outer garments before he could get up and walk. Once the last layer is removed, healing breaks forth. We need patience as God deals with each layer that may have in some way contributed to the symptoms.

Sins

Jesus healed many saying: 'Your sins are forgiven.' After He healed the crippled man, He told him to stop sinning or he would be worse off than before (John 5:14). Sin can cause sickness and disease. Where sin is the root, we simply need to confess the sin and ask for His forgiveness. Many may not acknowledge sin as being the cause of the symptoms, and hence refuse to address the underlying issues.

Unforgiveness

Sometimes, we may have to forgive before we are healed. We may have to forgive certain people, or our self, or God. God doesn't need to be forgiven, but we may feel a grudge or some disappointment towards God that we need to address. When we choose not to forgive, we remain in bondage. Many people have come to me with body pains where ordinary prayer has not worked. However, when I asked if they needed to forgive anyone, tears poured down their face. The moment they forgave, healing occurred.

Jesus said: *'Whenever you stand praying, forgive if you have anything against anyone, so that your Father in Heaven will also forgive you for your sins,'* (Mark 11:25). He also said to forgive from *the heart* (Matthew 18:35). This means we don't simply say: 'I forgive you' but we also say: *'I forgive you for... I choose to let you off the hook. You owe me nothing. I pray God will bless you...'* It is good to say the person's name and mention the things said or done or not done, that brought the pain or anger. Jesus said on the cross: *'Father, forgive them, for they know not what they do'.*

When we need to forgive, it is powerful if we imagine the person standing in front of us and look into their eyes. This makes it feel real and from the heart. It doesn't matter if the person is dead or alive. When we forgive from our hearts, we are the ones who are set free from spiritual bondage. If we need to forgive our self, it is good to look in a mirror and say to yourself, 'I forgive you'. Keep saying this until your heart responds. Then let yourself off the hook and choose not to punish yourself anymore. Know the truth that the Lord forgives those who repent from their heart and remembers their sins no more (Jeremiah 31:34). His forgiveness is like the waves of the sea washing over us. Just as the waves wash over the sand and remove all traces, so His forgiveness removes our sin and remembers it no more.

Witchcraft & the Occult

Sometimes, people's ongoing ill health may be due to witchcraft. I have seen this many times in Africa, though it may occur anywhere. Some people carry evil power to the extent that they can inflict sickness and death on others.

There was a woman who was struggling with chronic diarrhoea, losing weight and needed medical attention. She was from Europe and I felt to ask her if she had any enemies. She admitted there were a group of satanists or white witches who were after her. A group of us stood around her and took authority over the witchcraft, sickness and death. Her symptoms went and she made a recovery.

There was a devout African woman who fled to England who was actually a princess in her native country. She had a regal character and carried spiritual authority. She started to become unwell and her symptoms gradually got worse. She ended up in hospital and sadly never made it out. Everyone assumed she would be fine, because she carried such authority and had a warrior's heart. A group of us fasted and prayed for her healing. In the Spirit, we saw some of her native people coming against her by performing witchcraft and black magic. The battle was immense, and sadly we were not able to see the victory. I believe she was someone who was righteous and spared from more evil: *'The righteous perish and no-one ponders it in his heart; devout men are taken away to be spared from evil,'* (Isaiah 57:1).

We are not to fear witchcraft, satanists or the occult but be aware there are evil practices that can invoke sickness and even death. Some cases may need bringing before the Courts of Heaven, where we can ask God our Judge for mercy and justice, and freedom from high-ranking demonic powers.

Habitual Sin- A Change of Lifestyle

Habitual sins usually require a new lifestyle. A person can be healed of an addiction only to return to their sinful habit. The habitual pattern needs to be broken and the lifestyle changed so they move forward instead of turning back.

Habitual sins are cravings of the flesh that are constantly 'fed' by the sinful habit. If this part of the brain is no longer fed (by stopping the habit), then the wires forming the pathways will become weakened and cease. Instead, when a person develops a new behaviour, a new pathway will start to form in the brain.

The Lord always provides ways out. He is the way forward. He is to be the centre of our life. His truth sets us free. Unless we choose to hate the sin, we may struggle with temptation. We are not to live by the flesh but by the Spirit. A good question to ask is, where does the person want to be when they are sixty years of age? Only they can take responsibility for their choices in life. We are accountable to God for what we think and do, for He sees and knows everything. Nothing is hidden from Him. The enemy tries to fool us into thinking it is ok, no-one knows or God doesn't care, along with many other lies. *'For a man's ways are in full view of the Lord and He examines all his paths. He will die for lack of discipline, led astray by his own great folly,'* (Proverbs 5:21-23). We can't afford to be fooled any more by Satan's lies or temptations of the flesh. Habitual sins may be a cover up for wounded hearts, in which case inner healing and mentoring may be required.

Wounded Hearts
Another reason people are not healed is because they carry deep seated pain or emotional trauma. This can include abandonment and rejection. Wounded hearts are a common cause of many symptoms. This is discussed in more detail in Volume 3.

Lack of Knowledge
People perish from lack of knowledge (Hosea 5:6). There is a worldly saying, 'ignorance is bliss'. This may be true in some cases, thought it is a stumbling block if we're not aware of the enemy's schemes (2 Corinthians 2:11). Just as medical knowledge is required to heal the sick, spiritual knowledge is required to discern the roots to free people from bondage. Nowadays, I approach things differently compared to what I did years ago, simply because I have grown more in wisdom and understanding with regards to ministering healing and freedom.

Lack of Perseverance
Healing can be a process, a bit like peeling back the layers from an onion, until the core issue is addressed. Sometimes, we are to hold on in faith and trust He will heal. Other times we are to work through the issues or layers, one by one.

There was a testimony from Mahesh Chavda[1] of an old blind woman who came to one of his crusades for healing. Each time she went forward for prayer she fell to the floor as the Spirit came on her, but would get up still blind. This happened every night, and on the last night of the crusade, she not only fell to the ground but got up completely healed. When Mahesh asked the

Lord why this happened, the Lord showed him a picture of an octopus with its tentacles around this woman. Each time she fell down in the Spirit, one of the 'tentacles' was removed. Only when the last 'tentacle' was removed, she got up completely healed. Jesus said: '*Will not God bring about justice for His chosen ones who cry out to Him night and day? Will He keep putting them off? I tell you He will see that they get justice and quickly,*' (Luke 18:6).

Focus on Jesus, Not the Sickness

Many focus too much on the sickness or symptoms instead of on the Healer. If we look to Jesus, instead of moaning or self-pity (the pit of 'self' or 'woe is me'), then healing may follow. Jesus told people to step out, get up or reach out, in order to be healed. They had to look to Him and no longer focus on their sickness. This requires faith in Him and looking to Him instead of the sickness. Thanksgiving and praise are good tools to help turn our eyes to Jesus. Moaning achieves nothing for it is a pit of self. Paul chose to give thanks and praise in *all* his sufferings and trials, or near death experiences. He told the Thessalonians to do three things, and this can be seen as taking three medicines (1 Thessalonians 5:16):

1. *Be joyful always*
2. *Pray continually*
3. *Give thanks in all circumstances*

We are to fix our eyes on what is unseen, not what is seen (2 Corinthians 4:18). Through our eyes of faith, we can claim on earth what we see in Heaven. Hence we pray, 'Your will be done, on earth as in Heaven'. Unbelief focuses on the symptoms, whereas faith focuses on God and healing. God gives life to the dead and calls things that are not as though they were (Romans 4:17). This applies to people who have received healing and the symptoms later return. As long as they haven't turned back to sin or doubted the healing, they can reject the symptoms and by faith take back their rightful healing. Satan throws back the sickness to make us believe we were not healed. It is a trap and if we believe this lie, we will fall back. If we deal with the sin and stand firm on the faith that we have been healed, the sickness or symptoms will go.

Is it God's Will?

God is the God who heals, though a person's illness may lead to death. Sometimes, I may sense a person is not going to be healed, but God is waiting to take them to heaven. Other times, it may be a spiritual battle where I've felt led to pray and fast with others.

Some are aware their time on earth has finished and are ready for their spirit to depart. Others may have had out-of-body heavenly encounters and don't want their spirit to return to earth. Sometimes God may allow us to choose and other times He may not.

Does the Person Want to be Healed?

As strange as this may sound, there are people who don't want to be healed. Or they may want their symptoms to go but are not willing to deal with the underlying issues. Jesus asked the blind man what he wanted Him to do? (Luke 18:41). Surely, Jesus knew the man wanted his sight restored. However, some don't necessarily want to be healed as their sickness or disability is their identity and source of income.

We mustn't be discouraged if someone isn't initially healed but ask the Holy Spirit for wisdom and discernment as regards what to do next, or to expose any possible blockages.

END NOTES

[1] Chavda, Mahesh: *Hidden Power of Healing Prayer;* Destiny Image, (2011)

12

When You Fast

When you fast put oil on your head and wash your face,
so that it will not be obvious to men that you are fasting,
but only to your Father who is unseen

Matthew 6:17

The moment I felt called to serve God on the mission field, I somehow knew fasting was to become a part of my lifestyle. Since I could no longer avoid it, I decided to look for the reasons why we should fast. There are actually many reasons why we should fast. The enemy so discourages us from fasting because he doesn't want us to know the truth and power behind fasting, for it is one of the most powerful weapons for spiritual breakthrough.

Jesus didn't say, 'if' but *'when'* you fast (Matthew 6:16). Fasting was something the disciples were to do as part of life.

What is Fasting?

Fasting is when we choose to abstain from things that please or feed our flesh (body and soul). Instead, we choose to hunger for more of God by focusing on His Spirit. In effect, we are submitting the flesh (body and soul) to our spirit, and surrendering our spirit to God. When we fast, we are focusing on the spirit instead of the flesh, and this helps to tune our spirit to hear Him more clearly. Fasting is an important tool when seeking spiritual breakthrough, direction or simply more of God's presence. God's power can work through us in greater measure than before, as a result of fasting. Fasting is like a spiritual power drill to break through spiritually dry grounds so we can access the deeper living waters below.

Fasting was something I never wanted to do. However, I soon saw the importance it would play in my life when I realized it was a spiritual weapon. Fasting is recognized as one of the spiritual disciplines. The more we fast, the easier it becomes as our flesh yields to our spirit.

Reasons to Fast

Here are some of the reasons why we should fast.

It is a Command

When Jesus spoke to His disciples about fasting, He didn't say *'if'* but *'when'* you fast. '**When you fast** *put oil on your head and wash your face, so that it will not be obvious to men that you are fasting, but only to your Father who is unseen; and your Father,* **who sees what is done in secret, will reward you***,'* (Matthew 6:17). Father God rewards all who fast in secret. Jesus was questioned why the disciples didn't fast and replied: *'How can the guests of the Bridegroom mourn while He is with them? The time will come when the Bridegroom will be taken from them;* **then they will fast***,'* (Matthew 9:15).

When the Lord calls us to serve Him, fasting usually plays a role. This may be on a regular basis or for specific times and seasons. For some, this may be a day every week and for others, it may be three to five days a month or a month each year. It is between you and God how often you fast. When we fast on a regular basis, it helps our flesh come under the rule of our spirit and keeps us Spirit-focused instead of being ministry or flesh-focused. It is a bit like going to the gym to keep our bodies fit. Fasting helps to keep our spirit healthy and yielded to God.

Fasting is one of the main spiritual disciplines. We are showing the enemy we are not under the rulership of our flesh or the world, but God. Changes are coming, and fasting will help prepare our spirits to be ready for when they come.

Spiritual Breakthrough

When Jesus reached thirty years of age, He began His ministry with a forty-day fast. This fast was God ordained as the Spirit led Him into the wilderness. During the fast, Jesus was able to overcome all trials and temptations, as a result of Him focusing on God and His Word. Jesus was challenged with the same tests and temptations the Israelites faced when they were in the desert, but He passed them all. After achieving this spiritual breakthrough, He was ready to enter His ministry, but now in the *power* of the Spirit.

This was a significant season of spiritual breakthrough where Jesus overcame the tests and trials of the enemy. Fasting is an excellent tool or spiritual weapon, for breakthrough in our lives, as well as seeing breakthrough in the lives of others.

Whenever I feel my spiritual journey has reached a plateau, or I'm not sure where things are going, then I choose to fast. Through fasting we humble ourselves before God, knowing our need of Him in our lives. It reveals how desperate we are for Him.

One time, during a season of transition, I felt desperate to know where God was in my life. So I fasted as my spirit cried out to Him, and I continued until He answered and revealed Himself to me. Suddenly, on the third day, I was overwhelmed with His loving presence. It was as if His presence invaded the room and overshadowed me. It felt as if the 'power drill' effect of fasting had struck water or oil, because after this my relationship with God was at a deeper level.

Fasting is like a power drill in the ground. It breaks the impenetrable rock until breakthrough occurs and fresh water or oil comes gushing forth from the ground.

Daniel was a man of prayer and fasting. When he saw God was grieved by the sins of the people, he responded with prayer and fasting (Daniel 9:3-16). After Daniel's vision concerning a great war, he prayed and fasted for three weeks. During this fast, he ate no choice food, or meat or wine (Daniel 10:2-3). From day one of his fast, God's warring angels were doing battle in the

Heavenly realms. As he fasted for twenty-one days, his prayers caused a powerful ripple effect in the heavenly realms between the Kingdom of God and satan. There was a tremendous battle between the Archangel Michael and the principality over the Persian region. Finally, the angel who had been waging war in the heavenly realms arrived and said: '*The prince of the Persian kingdom resisted me twenty-one days. Then Michael, one of the chief princes, came to help me, because I was detained there with the prince of Persia*' (Daniel 10:13). It took twenty-one days of spiritual warfare through prayer and fasting to break through the demonic strongholds over the nation.

A 'Daniel fast' refers to a partial fast, such as a single meal a day, or just having fruit, bread, soup or vegetables. There is no choice food such as meat, wine or other enjoyable ingredients.

There was a time when I felt immense spiritual opposition to my calling and ministry. What I sensed in the spirit was confirmed by a word from a credible prophet. The prophet said, 'Just like Daniel fasted for twenty-one days and the arch-angel Michael came to intercept against the prince of Persia, the Lord will wage war on your behalf and end the tug of war in the spirit realm.' After hearing this, I felt prompted to go on a Daniel fast. Two days after the fast had finished, I was invited to a special conference with anointed believers. At the end of this special gathering, I knew the battle was finally over.

Fasting can be a way to see breakthrough in our ministry, health, families, churches or even nations. When people ask me to pray for them to see a breakthrough in their health or life, I usually invite them to fast, because I believe it's fasting that releases breakthrough.

As well as individual fasts, there can be corporate fasts. Corporate fasts are when groups of believers come together in prayer and fasting to see breakthrough. Esther arranged a corporate fast where she and her people fasted for three days to deliver the Jews from the clutches of death (Esther 4:12-16).

I signed up to take part in a fifty-day church fast where people took it in turns to pray and fast each day. The results were amazing. There was a shift in prayer and worship, as the believers had caught something during this season of pressing in deeper through prayer and fasting.

Satanists fast in order to gain greater demonic power for spiritual breakthrough. However, their breakthrough is in the demonic realm. They pray and fast to see families break up, divorces take place and to bring destruction, even death, on people, churches or ministries. If they fast to gain demonic power, think how much more powerful it is when Christians fast to bring Kingdom breakthrough in people's lives, or churches and nations! Fasting is a powerful tool that we are no longer to ignore.

Healing & Deliverance

I believe fasting is essential for anyone involved in healing and deliverance ministry. Fasting is like moving up in gears when contending for breakthrough.

Fasting releases miracles. The demon behind the epilepsy would only come out with prayer and *fasting* (Mathew 17:14-21). The famous Smith Wigglesworth was asked to pray for a Welsh man who was dying of Tuberculosis. He did, but the man wasn't healed. As Wigglesworth was walking up the Welsh mountains, the Lord told him to go back and pray for this man. This time he fasted and asked a group of fellow elders to join him in fasting and prayer. As he fasted, he came up against the demon that was behind the disease. The symptoms of TB came upon Smith Wigglesworth himself and he spent the night battling in the spirit until it finally left him. He overcame the spirit behind the man's TB through fasting and prayer. When he went back to the man who was dying, he and the fellow believers followed the Lord's strategy. They simply joined hands around the man and said one word, 'Jesus'. They quietly repeated the name Jesus until the man had an encounter with Jesus and jumped off the bed, healed and set free.[1]

Fasting may be required before we minister, whether to an individual or to a corporate body of believers. It prepares our hearts and finer tunes our spirit to hear God and minister under His anointing. People may fast before ministering at conferences. Some fast for weeks beforehand, since battles are going on and the enemy is trying to stop the move of the Spirit or people coming.

159

Prayer and fasting release supernatural power and can create an open heaven for God's angels and Spirit to come in power during a conference. I have noticed the difference when attending conferences where there has been prayer and fasting beforehand compared to conferences where there has been little or none. Miracles, healings and heavenly encounters are the norm where prayer and fasting has prepared the way for the Lord to come.

Sanctify Ourselves Before Engaging in Battle

Joshua told the people to consecrate themselves before they crossed the Jordan (Joshua 3:5). It may be right to fast before entering or engaging in a spiritual battle. Through fasting, we sanctify our body, soul and spirit as we yield every part of our self to the Lord.

Holy Communion is another way to sanctify ourselves as we partake in the body and blood of Jesus. Many take Communion on a daily basis when fasting. There is power in the Communion and it can prepare our spirits for the battles ahead (more is discussed in Volume two).

Battles are to be fought in the Spirit-realm and not in the flesh (Ephesians 6:12). Hence, we prepare by humbling ourselves, knowing the battle is the Lord's and we are under His authority and guidance (2 Chronicles 20:15). Pride has no place in spiritual warfare. We will fall if we fight with pride or in our own strength. Since the battle is spiritual, this means we rely on God's army of angels and Heavenly beings to fight for us.

On one occasion, God called me to engage in a battle I didn't want to get involved in, but rather flee. I've come to realize God sometimes assigns us to do things we don't want to do, so we are totally dependent on Him for the task. (However, He may assign us to what we want to do because He has prepared our hearts for it.) It was during the week before New Year at a mission base in Africa, when I started to sense an evil presence in the atmosphere outside our base. It was getting thicker each day and I just wanted to get on a plane and flee to England for a break. God had other plans. He told me I was to stay and pray around the base during this time leading up to New Year, for I was here for such a time as this. I reluctantly obeyed, then found out He had also called others to stay and intercede for the area and base. God doesn't usually ask us to do things alone but will connect us with others whom He has also called to pray. I heard there were many witchdoctors, sorcerers and shamanists attending a New Year celebration just across the road from us. This was a time when they would engage with water spirits and demonic powers so they could receive greater measures of evil power. God called us to stand against these evil forces and we responded to what the Holy Spirit directed us to do.

As we began praying, some of us felt led to fast for the week. It was amazing how God gave me grace to fast during this time, for He removed my desire to eat. I was not hungry during the fast and my appetite returned when it was over. We consecrated ourselves before God, repented of all known sin (so we had no open door to sin by which the enemy could attack us), and worshipped and prayed around our base, as well as for the area. As we met to pray on New Year's Eve, I prayed God would release thunder and lightning down from Heaven. I had never prayed this before but felt led by the Spirit to do so. At that moment in time there was clear blue sky and not a cloud in sight. Within a few hours a storm started to brew. This was no ordinary storm. There came strong winds with terrifying thunder and lightning. It was one of the most powerful and terrifying storms I have witnessed. The next day we heard reports, that the satanists and witchdoctors were furious for their plans had been thwarted. One of them even commented that they saw power coming from our base which had stopped them using their powers. It was amazing to see what God did. The following year the witchdoctors and Satanists decided not to return to the same place but sought somewhere else to go. The next New Year was peaceful and there was no oppression sensed in the atmosphere.

Through fasting, we not only purify ourselves and close any open doors in our heart to the enemy, but we humbly posture ourselves under the leadership and authority of the Lord.

Benefits of Fasting

There are many benefits to fasting. We benefit physically and spiritually when we choose to fast. Here are some of the benefits.

Healthier Bodies

In the natural, when we fast our bodies undergo a process of detoxification. One or two days fast every week has been scientifically proven to be beneficial to our health. If our bodies undergo a detoxification and clean up, then our spirits are undergoing a similar process of sanctification. Fasting enables us to become holy vessels where God can release greater power and anointing for the work He has commissioned us to do.

Daniel and his men were healthy and strong when they fasted from meat and wine during their partial fast. *'At the end of the ten days they looked healthier and better nourished than any of the young men who ate the royal food,'* (Daniel 1:15).

Pre-operation Preparation

I usually advise people to fast before they come to receive inner healing ministry. This is because I don't want them to be dependent upon me, but to take responsibility for themselves by showing God how seriously they want to be healed and set free. It is a bit like the preparation before a surgical operation, where people are told to fast (not to eat or drink anything for a certain time before the operation). Those who are unable to fast from food can do a partial fast or fast from other things such as TV, alcohol, social media or whatever takes up a chunk of their time. As they fast, the can prepare their heart, mind and spirit to become more receptive to the Lord.

One lady decided to fast before we met for prayer. She had an amazing download from the Lord concerning the spiritual and emotional roots behind her symptoms. As a result, she came spiritually prepared for the ministry.

Increase in Spiritual Authority

During a fast, God does a deeper, sanctifying work in our hearts, which in turn releases more of His authority to overcome the enemy. Fasting releases spiritual authority. Our spirit grows in authority when we yield our flesh to God and let Him be Lord in our life. As we fast from our flesh, our spirit becomes sharper and more sensitive to the promptings of the Holy Spirit. Whereas food and drink can dull the spirit, fasting can sharpen the spirit.

Spiritual Direction

Fasting helps to direct our path when we are seeking spiritual direction. We are tuning our spiritual senses to hear, see and sense or discern more clearly. I have benefitted from fasting when seeking God's will or way forward. He has replied to my hunger and desire to do His will, by revealing the next steps.

While the church at Antioch were praying and fasting, the Lord spoke to them and said: '*Set apart for me Saul and Barnabas for the work to which I have called them*' (Acts 13:2). Here prayer and fasting released a calling and commissioning. People can hear God more clearly when praying together in the unity of the Spirit. Jesus said when two or more come together in His Name, He is with them (Matthew 18:20).

Overcome Temptation

Fasting helps to resist or overcome temptation. Jesus fasted in the desert and resisted all temptation from satan. Temptation speaks to the flesh. Hence, when we fast and surrender our flesh to our spirit, we are saying 'no' to temptation.

I would automatically turn on the TV every evening when I came back from work, to help relax and unwind. This seemed a normal part of life until I took a sabbatical, and the Lord asked me to fast from TV for six weeks. At the end of the six weeks, I turned on the TV and realized how much rubbish was on it and how it polluted my mind and dulled my spirit. I saw how my spiritual senses had become sharper and clearer during the fast, hence chose to watch little TV from then on.

Supernatural Food

Jesus told His disciples about there being supernatural food in the Kingdom: '*I have food to eat that you know nothing about,*' (John 4:32). '*Man doesn't live on bread alone but on every word which comes from the mouth of God,*' (Matthew 4:4). Jesus has supernatural food, manna from Heaven, which will sustain us and supply the power and energy our body needs. He said to the ones who overcame the teachings of Balaam and the Nicolaitans: *'I will give you some of the hidden manna,'* (Revelation 2:17).

There are testimonies of people who have stayed alive by simply taking Communion and eating nothing else. There is a mystery behind fasting and taking Communion that we are not to ignore.

Types of Fasting

There are many types of fasting, but the three most common ones mentioned in the scriptures are; *total fast, food fast and partial fasts.* We can ask the Holy Spirit what type of fast to do and how long to fast.

Complete Fasts

A complete or total fast means no food and no drink. A total fast is usually no more than three days long, for there is a risk of the kidneys going into failure if a person has no fluid for more than seventy two hours. The best example is when Esther did a three day complete fast, abstaining from food and drink (Esther 4:16).

Food Fasts

The next fasts are food fasts, where food is abstained but drinks are allowed. Some may only drink water or gradually wean from taking juices and hot drinks to just water. This can be from a day to up to forty days, though some may fast for longer. It is wise to be Spirit-led if you are thinking of doing a long fast or get a medical check beforehand if there are any health issues. Some may take a piece of bread or fruit if their sugar levels start to feel low or they become dizzy. It is good to drink less caffeine before and during any fast to prevent having headaches, which are the result of the withdrawal effects of caffeine.

It is my understanding that Jesus probably fasted from food, but not water, when in the desert. Some may disagree, but scriptures only mention Him not eating food, being tempted with food and feeling extremely hungry at the end. There is nothing that says He fasted from water, or was thirsty, or tempted with water. Strictly speaking, He would be dead if He fasted from water for more than four days, unless He was supernaturally sustained. Since He came to show us the way to follow, it makes sense He fasted from food but not water.

Partial Fasts or Daniel Fasts

A partial fast is where food is fasted from in part. Some may have one meal a day or just soup with bread. Others abstain from certain foods in their diet such as meat, alcohol, desserts, or they may choose to just eat salads, fruit or vegetables. A Daniel fast is the best example of a partial fast, where he only ate vegetables and abstained from meat and alcohol. Some people choose a partial or Daniel fast for health reasons, or because they need some energy sustenance for their daily physical demands.

Other Fasts

For those who struggle or are unable to fast from food, there are other fasts such as abstaining from TV, sports or games, personal interests, social media, etc. A fast that is beneficial to everyone is a fast from 'negative speech'. I encourage you to do this if you haven't already done one. Fast for a month from saying negative speech. This means resisting criticism, judgement, gossip, moaning, disapproval, complaining or pessimistic speech. Things may start to shift in us as we choose to give thanks and praise, and to bless or pray for our enemies. It helps us see things from God's perspective. It is a great spiritual exercise to help a person break free from negative speech.

Fasting is beneficial to our body, soul and spirit. It can release healing, as well as spiritual breakthrough, and also draws us closer to God.

END NOTES

[1] Roberts, Liardon: *Smith Wigglesworth Prayer, Power and Miracles*; p 204-7, Destiny Image Publishers (2005).
[2] Chavda, Mahesh: *The Hidden Power of Prayer and Fasting.* Destiny Image Publishers (1998)

13

Deliverance Guidelines

God anointed Jesus of Nazareth with the Holy Spirit and power
and He went around healing all who were under the power of the devil,
because God was with Him

Acts 10:38

As I stepped onto African soil in 2006, I was an apprentice when it came to divine healthcare. At the beginning of this adventure with God, the Holy Spirit asked if He could join me in the medical consultations. I was overwhelmed and humbled by His gentlemanly approach. In hindsight, He was humbly inviting me to co-labour with Him. I immediately made room for Him, not knowing how much I was going to need Him. He was like a gentleman as He faithfully stood beside me, teaching me what I needed to know for the various medical cases. He is the best counselor who gives us clues to the issues behind symptoms and teaches us the right way to minister healing, whether by giving medicines, practical advice, or through prayer.

There are different ways God can set us free. People may be healed and set free during worship, or when taking Communion. Some are healed through encountering God in dreams. Others are healed or set free when a case is presented before the Courts of Heaven. One of the best ways God can restore our souls is when we soak in His presence. David said: '*The Lord is My Shepherd... He makes me lie down in green pastures and leads me besides still waters. He restores my soul*' (Psalm 23:1-2).

Here are some guidelines for deliverance but the best guide is to be led by the Holy Spirit and not simply copy what others do. The Holy Spirit is our number one counselor and will always guide us with wisdom as to what to do, as I have witnessed countless times myself. We simply invite Him to be with us instead of doing it with our flesh. I honour the Holy Spirit for teaching me and guiding me in healing and deliverance. Without Him being beside me, I couldn't have done it.

Do You Need to be Born-again to Receive Deliverance?

This is one of the questions people ask. I would like to answer by referring to both experience and the Word of God. Jesus didn't tell anyone that they had to become a follower of His before He healed them. To some, like the cripple at the pool, He later explained he would be worse if he continued to sin (John 5:14). The lady who had been crippled by a spirit for eighteen years, Jesus simply freed her from the spirit of infirmity (Luke 13:11).

While it is Biblically acceptable to heal and deliver a person without them stepping into the Kingdom of God, it is recommended that they accept Jesus as their Lord and Saviour, ideally before or after they have been delivered. The reason isn't one of religion or forcing others to be Christians, but there is wisdom in it and future protection for the person.

Jesus addressed this in Luke 11:24. He said: '*When an evil spirit comes out of a man, it goes through arid places seeking rest and does not find it. Then it says, "I will return to the house I left". When it arrives it finds the house swept clean and put in order. Then it goes and takes seven other spirits more wicked than itself, and they go in and live there. And the final condition of the man is worse than the first*'. Here, Jesus is referring to our bodies as spiritual temples and when we command an evil spirit to leave, we need to invite the Holy Spirit to fill that 'empty' place so no other evil spirits worse than the first can enter into the 'spiritually clean house'.

I have seen people healed and delivered without accepting Jesus in their lives. This has especially been on the mission field when I have ministered to people of other faiths and God simply wanted me to love them and pray for their physical needs, including setting them free. However, other times I have felt led to draw people into the Kingdom of God first (through inviting Jesus into their lives), before delivering them from evil spirits.

There was an African lady who started to demonically manifest when she received prayer for her body pain. She started to lose consciousness as her eyes rolled back, and her body began to violently shake. At this point, I took authority over the demon by binding the evil spirit, and then commanded her to come back to consciousness in Jesus' Name. A minute or so later, she regained her consciousness, and I then felt led to introduce her to Jesus. She agreed to accept Jesus into her life. After accepting Jesus, she was in a position of spiritual authority to renounce the evil spirit herself. As she renounced the spirit, she was delivered with no further manifestations, and her body pain was healed.

Demons manifest because they do not want to leave a body and feel threatened when someone prays for them to leave. They try to take over the person's consciousness, especially in someone who hasn't been born again or received the Holy Spirit. This is to prevent them renouncing the demon. It is easier to deliver someone from a demonic spirit when the person is willing to take responsibility. By this I mean, the person repents and commands the evil spirit(s) to leave their body. It is usually cast out with minor or no manifestations when it is done this way. If the person doesn't want the evil spirit(s) to leave, then I don't think there is much point in praying for them. This is because it may start to manifest, and there will be a battle for it to come out. Likewise, if it does leave the person, there is a high chance it will re-enter again unless the person repents and changes their lifestyle.

God may lead us to set people free and then introduce them to Jesus. However, we need to be wise and obedient to whatever the Spirit is telling us to do at that moment in time.

Manifestations

Manifestations can come from three sources: *the Holy Spirit, the demonic or the flesh.*

169

Demonic Manifestations

As already mentioned, when a demonic spirit is aroused it may start to manifest, especially if it is under threat of being cast out of someone's body. However, it is true to say people can be delivered without any manifestations at all.

Manifestations of demonic spirits can be minor or major. Minor ones include feelings of nausea, vomiting, sneezing, yawning, burping (usually a foul smell comes out), spitting, sighing, fluttering of eyes, tear formation, coughing, hot and cold sensations, dizziness or sudden headaches. The demons may leave through orifices in the body and the individual then starts feeling better or comments on having 'felt something leave their body' from the area affected. Sometimes people may feel worse during prayer and this is simply because a spirit has been aroused. We can ask the Holy Spirit for further revelation and guidance as to how to free the person, or perhaps refer them to someone else if you feel out of your depth.

Major manifestations may include violent actions, writhing about on the floor like a snake, fits, change of voice (usually deep and evil sounding), screams, hissing noises, foul language, rolled back eyes and loss of consciousness. The person may not be aware of a major manifestation after it has occurred as the demonic spirit may take over their conscious mind and body.

It's important to keep on loving the person as you take authority over the demon and calmly bind it in Jesus' Name, commanding it to be quiet and stop manifesting. If they are losing consciousness or become unconscious, then bind the spirit and command them to come back to conscious level in Jesus' Name. Command them to open their eyes if shut. It can be good to look directly into their eyes when commanding the demonic spirit to be quiet or leave. Also, get them into a more comfortable upright position if not already in one. Then you can lead them into repentance prayer (and ideally to accept Jesus in their lives if they haven't already done so) before getting them to take responsibility and renounce the spirit for themselves. I believe one of the reasons people lose consciousness when they are demonically manifesting is that the demon doesn't want to leave and tries to take control of their mind and body.

If the person is struggling to be set free, then you can decide to do one of two things. You can stop going any further and pray a blessing over them, before seeking help from others more experienced in this area of ministry. Or you can ask the Holy Spirit for further revelation and wisdom into what is happening or hindering the deliverance, and where next to direct the prayers.

Sometimes, you may be dealing with emotional hurts and pain, and other times there may be a cluster of demons that need to come out one by one. Spiritual discernment is needed to deal with such cases that are not straightforward since every case will be different for each person.

Just as Jesus sent His disciples out in twos to minister to the sick, so it is wise to have another relatively experienced Christian alongside you when doing healing and deliverance ministry (unless you are very experienced yourself or are training others in the ministry). If I have no alternative, then I may pray for people on my own but I usually seek an assistant if possible. This is important especially if I am praying for someone of the opposite sex. This is to minimise any counterattacks from the enemy, and it is helpful to have another person bear witness and discern what is happening to the person receiving the ministry.

Holy Spirit Manifestations

When a person experiences the Holy Spirit, they may feel lighter in their bodies and sense the peace, joy or love of God. Other manifestations of the Holy Spirit include feeling hot and sweaty (I have seen some perspire greatly with droplets of sweat falling down their body when receiving the fire of the Holy Spirit). Also, there may be fluttering eyes or tears of joy. Some experience a tingling sensation, others feel rods of electricity through their body. Some feel weak at the legs and want to lie or fall down, others break into holy laughter. Some may roar like a lion or make other funny noises, or start to shake as the Holy Spirit is on them. All this is good when God is moving and doing a deeper work. Some people experience no manifestations, but the Holy Spirit is powerfully with them.

Manifestations are no indication of depth of intimacy with God. Some well-known anointed leaders rarely manifest when the anointing of the Holy Spirit is on them.

Flesh Manifestations

I have seen some amazing manifestations of the flesh when the person has been in a frenzied or 'unconscious' mode. In each situation, the person is usually seeking attention or wanting an audience, hence it will occur where there are many people around. Spiritual discernment is needed and the best way to manage is to either get everyone to leave and ignore the person, or to gently whisper in the ear to stop and get up.

On one occasion, whilst on mission, I was asked to go and see a visitor who was unconscious on the floor. As I went, the room was full of spectators who were all worried and concerned about the person who appeared to be unconscious. There was a visiting doctor who was keen to do the emergency medical intervention for someone unconscious. However, after an initial examination noting her clinical observations were normal, I had a check in my spirit that there was something else going on. I realised the incident happened when the room was full of onlookers. I quietly asked all the visitors to step outside and the visiting doctor to hold back for a moment. We stopped giving attention to the person and just quietly observed outside the room. Within minutes, the person regained consciousness and was looking around to see who was there. No medical intervention was needed. It turned out after further questioning that the person had significant emotional and spiritual issues that needed addressing. This was a non-organic case that didn't require medical intervention but rather inner healing.

There needs to be spiritual discernment for any manifestation witnessed. Is this an evil spirit which needs to be bound and cast out? Is it the Holy Spirit ministering to the person? Or, is the person simply faking it and wanting attention? If it is the latter, then we just need to quietly whisper in their ear that they can stop what they are doing and get up, or take them to a quiet place where there is less attention. A person may be delivered of a demon without any manifestation, just like a person can be filled with the Holy Spirit without any manifestation.

Useful Guidelines

Here are some useful guidelines I would like to share that I have learnt over the years.

Should We Get Involved?

We must discern if we should get involved with those who need ministry. Sometimes we are not to get involved and are to leave it to others whom God has appointed. Other times we may need to fast and pray beforehand. Some people may want to be healed from a sickness but are unwilling to acknowledge and renounce the spirit behind it. In this case, I would bless them and not minister any further without their co-operation in the matter. It is difficult to help anyone who isn't willing to help themselves or take responsibility for their own problems. All they may do is drain those who minister to them. Wisdom and grace are needed when to help and in what capacity or whether to leave alone or refer to others.

Speaking with Authority

Sometimes, when individuals receiving ministry start to manifest a demon, those around may start shouting at the demon from a place of fear. I don't believe this is healthy for those praying or the individual receiving prayer. I would suggest taking the individual into a more relaxed and peaceful environment with only a few there to minister from a place of authority and love. Shouting at demons doesn't release spiritual authority, especially when the shouting is caused by fear arising within those praying for the individual. However, a quiet voice that carries authority can bind and cast out a manifesting spirit. Jesus didn't shout at demons but He commanded them to be quiet and leave, by speaking with authority.

I was asked to go and help a teenager who was apparently 'fitting' on the floor and unresponsive to those who were shouting at the demon to leave. As I went, I immediately thought the 'fits' weren't genuine and the person appeared to be in a panic-like mode. The person didn't respond to my advice, so I knelt by their side and whispered in their ear telling the spirit to stop manifesting and for the person to come back into conscious mode. Within seconds, the person opened their eyes and sat up again.

We need to carry God's love and to not fear any demon we encounter or manifestation we see, for He that is in us is greater than he that is in the world (1 John 4:4). As we carry His love and presence, fear will leave, for perfect love casts out fear (1 John 4:18).

Jesus said: '*Do not be afraid, I am the First and the Last. I am the Living One; I was dead and behold I am alive forever and ever! And I hold the keys of death and Hades*' (Revelations 1:18). Jesus shared in our humanity, '*So that by His death, He might destroy him who holds the power of death, that is the devil, and free those who were held in slavery all their lives by their fear of death*' (Hebrews 2:14-15).

Demons will only submit to the Name of Jesus if the person speaking carries the authority of Jesus. Demons don't submit to fear, but authority. This was witnessed when some Jews who didn't know Jesus or have a relationship with Him, tried to drive out evil spirits by copying what the disciples did. They subsequently became victimised themselves when the evil spirit saw they had no authority to cast them out. '*Some Jews who went around driving out evil spirits tried to invoke the Name of the Lord Jesus over those who were demon-possessed. They would say, "**In the Name of Jesus whom Paul preaches, I command you to come out.**" Seven sons of Sceva, a Jewish chief priest, were doing this. One day the **evil spirit answered them, "Jesus I know and I know about Paul, but who are you?**" Then the man who had the evil spirit jumped on them and overpowered them all. He gave them such a beating that they ran out of the house naked and bleeding*' (Acts 19:13).

There is power in the Name of Jesus if the person speaking has His Spirit and authority. Authority comes out of our relationship with God. He releases more authority the further we choose to grow in our love-relationship with Him.

The higher the call on our lives, the greater the cost and personal sacrifice, and there will be greater authority for those who have laid down their lives for Him.

Jesus lived a life which was 100% human and 100% filled with the Spirit of God. He chose not to sin, though just like us, He was tempted in every way. He suffered no sickness or disease or ever allowed an evil spirit to enter Himself. He said that the prince of this world had no *hold* over Him (John 14:30).

As Christians, we can still have ungodly spirits in us, such as the spirit of pride, fear, sexual sin, jealousy and so on. Jesus was the only one who was without sin because He was the Son of God and conceived from the Holy Spirit (Matthew 1:20). It is not true to think we are demon free the moment we invite Jesus into our heart. The truth is, deliverance is an ongoing process in all of us because we all fall short and sin and have to deal with hurt, unforgiveness, control, pride, doubt and fear in our everyday lives. Jesus rebuked Satan from Peter just after Peter had the revelation that Jesus was the Son of God. He also rebuked His disciples from wanting to bring fire down to destroy the Samaritan village (Luke 9:55, Mark 8:33). Paul said: *'For God did not give us a **spirit of timidity**, but a **spirit of power, of love and self-discipline**,'* (2 Timothy 1:7).

However, Spirit-filled Christians will not become 'possessed' by demonic spirits unless they allow the demonic spirits to rule and reign in them. As long as we let God be our Lord and Saviour and reign in our hearts, then we will not become 'demon-possessed'. Believers can (unknowingly) allow evil spirits into their being, through social media, TV, films, alternative complementary medicines, or through being with others who carry spirits such as lust, pride, vanity, greed, judgment and so on. It is important to cleanse ourselves regularly with the blood of Jesus as we repent of such sin and hence close any doors in our heart we may have opened to the enemy (1 John 1:7-9).

Minister in Love

Healing is about being sensitive to the emotional part of a person's heart and not just focusing on the deliverance aspect. Jesus ministered with compassion, even when He cast out demons. We mustn't come under the fear of demons, but carry the Father's love for His children. Those who know their true identity as sons and daughters of their heavenly Father carry His heart of love and fearlessly reach out to others. If the person is feeling fear or angst, then quietly bind that spirit of fear and welcome the love and peace of God in their hearts before going further. Sometimes, it is best to minister first to the wounded heart before setting free from demons. With this approach, the demons may spontaneously flee when the person has an encounter with God.

There was an African lady who came to see me for treatment of her shaking arm. She came with fear and wanted medicines but no prayer. I quietly prayed against the spirit of fear and asked the Lord to release His peace. Within seconds she started to smile as the fear left and she allowed me to pray. I sensed she had been heavily involved in witchcraft, and after she repented of this, her shaking gradually reduced over the next few hours until it stopped completely, and she left healed.

Don't Minister in Areas You haven't Overcome
We can only help others in areas we have overcome or where the issue has never been a personal problem. How can someone help another out of the pit when they are in the pit? The moment we overcome an issue, we have authority to help others overcome. It's a bit like climbing a mountain where we can only help others in areas we have already mastered.

Laying on of Hands
The laying on of hands has become widely accepted in the healing ministry. However, we should respect a person's body and ask their permission. I don't think Jesus went around forcing His hands on people's heads. He would respect the individual and touch if appropriate. Jesus didn't always lay His hands on the sick, because it wasn't needed. It is best to be guided by the Spirit and be sensitive to each person. In some cases it is best not to touch, especially where there has been abuse and the person may feel uncomfortable. In other cases, it may be right to hold the person's hands. I only lay my hands on their head if the problem is around the head or if the Holy Spirit prompts me. We should respect the other person's body and only touch if led to do so. If I sense I'm to lay my hand on the part of the body that is sick, I ask

their permission and for them to put their hand over the area first, then I place my hand over theirs. This should be avoided if the issue is in a sensitive or private part of the body. Sometimes it may be right to kneel down instead of stand over someone, especially if they are elderly or of small stature. We should be sensitive to the Spirit and to those to whom we minister.

Hold no Grudges
It is wise to have peace and grace in our hearts before we pray for someone, and make sure we are not holding grudges or negative attitudes. This is so we minister from a heart of compassion and humility. It also prevents us from receiving anything from the enemy. Grudges, pride and an ungodly attitude will provide an open door for the enemy to come in. We can close doors to the enemy by choosing to minister from a heart of grace and love.

Pray with our Eyes Open
It is wise to pray with our eyes open so we do not get hit by the person if they start to manifest and lash out. Also, we can see into their spirit as we look into their eyes or observe their body response to what is going on. It takes practice to learn to see in the spirit with our eyes open. Also, our prayer partner may want to communicate to us and we won't see them if our eyes are shut.

Pain that Moves or Worsens
Something useful to know when ministering is if the symptoms, especially pain, begin to worsen or shift to another part of the body. In this case, you are most likely dealing with a demonic spirit. This would not happen in the natural, but it is a spiritual response to prayer. Either ask the Holy Spirit what the spirit represents or let the person receiving the ministry take responsibility by renouncing the spirit behind the symptoms.

End of Session
When the ministry is finished, we can ask the Holy Spirit to fill the person to overflowing with His peace and love. We can pray a blessing on them and seal all that has taken place with the blood of Jesus.

Prayer Before Ministry

If you have a prayer partner, then it is good to pray for each other and commit the ministry session to the Lord, by humbly submitting to His leadership and guidance. It is good to ask God for words of knowledge or revelation concerning what is going on or how to approach the matter. Sometimes, we may need to bind certain spirits before a session starts, so they don't manifest or cause distraction. This may be the spirit of deception, lies, fear, miscommunication, and so on. Also, remember to cover yourself and protect the session, by coming under the power of His blood. This is to hide the session from the enemy and minimize any backlash or counter attack afterwards.

Cleansing Before and After Ministry

It is important to be a clean, holy vessel for the Holy Spirit before we start ministering to others. In the same way we clean our hands before we medically treat a person, so we can spiritually cleanse ourselves before ministering. Hence, we can start by asking Jesus to cleanse and protect us with His blood. It is good to make sure your heart is at peace and carrying God's compassion and grace instead of any judgment, stress or feeling of unease. Otherwise we may find ourselves becoming sick, or taking on similar symptoms to the person receiving the ministry. Even if this were to happen, we can still repent of our wrongful attitude and ask Jesus to cleanse us with His blood.

At other times when I have been less prepared, I have simply said a quiet prayer putting the blood of Jesus between me and the person receiving the ministry. On one occasion, I silently prayed the blood of Jesus between me and a woman receiving deliverance, but my colleague didn't cover herself. As a result, I felt fine afterwards, but my colleague felt strange with a feeling of heaviness and oppression. After praying for my colleague and cleansing her with the blood, she felt fine again. If there has been little time to prepare or pray before ministering to someone, then I quickly cover myself with the blood of Jesus. This is a bit like putting on gloves before doing minor surgery. His blood covers and protects us from any contact with unclean spirits.

In the same way we cleanse ourselves before ministering, we also need to cleanse ourselves in body, soul and spirit *after* having ministered. It is like washing the hands after a medical procedure. It is good to ask the Holy Spirit to cleanse us from any unclean spirit(s) we may have come across, in the Name of Jesus. I call it 'de-sliming', that is, getting rid of any slime we may have picked up. This has proven to be effective prayer for protecting me and the team before and after ministry sessions.

Sometimes, it may be good to cleanse the room where you are ministering, both before and after the session. This keeps it sanctified allowing no unwanted 'filth' or 'unclean spirits' to hover around.

These are simply guidelines and the best teacher is the Holy Spirit. Remember we are students for life, and God can reveal more as we choose to depend on Him. He doesn't heal everyone with the same problem the same way. Jesus healed the five blind men in different ways. He healed the man who was born blind by putting mud mixed with saliva on the man's eyes, then telling him to wash his eyes in a pool (John 9:6). The blind beggar who cried out was instantly healed. Jesus said: *'Receive your sight; your faith has healed you'* (Luke 18:35-43). The blind man at Bethsaida was healed after Jesus spat on the man's eyes and laid His hands on them. This took two attempts (Mark 8:22-26). The two blind men who were sitting on the road side cried out to Jesus as He passed by. Jesus had compassion and touched their eyes and they were healed (Math 20:29-34).

A friend prophesied these words: *'When you think you know it, it is then that you don't. And when you think you don't know it, it is then that you do.'* This was a loving reminder of how we can't do anything without God's Holy Spirit and He loves it when we hold onto His hand and ask Him to lead the way.

14

Staying Healed

See, you are well again. Stop sinning or something
worse may happen to you

John 5:14

It is one thing to *be* healed and another to *stay* healed. Many who receive healing may encounter the same issue again. Why? There are different reasons. It is important to advise them how to stay healed by avoiding the sin or changing their lifestyle. Or it may simply be they need to stand on the truth of the healing they received.

Change of Lifestyle

Some illnesses are the result of habits or unhealthy lifestyles. Hence, in order to stay free, the habit or lifestyle needs to be changed. This applies to addictive lifestyles where the habit needs to stop in order to stay healed. True repentance is choosing not to go back to former habits or sins and to go in the opposite direction. Those who have succumbed to addictions must do what is necessary to prevent coming under the addiction again. They need to get rid of anything linked with the addiction, such as access to drugs, alcohol or porn, or no longer connect with those who encourage the addiction.

It is not enough to repent and still enjoy the habit. We need to hate the sin more than the pleasure we gain from it, otherwise we can be easily tempted back during vulnerable moments. The late Derek Prince testified to an area in his life where he struggled to be set free. He would repent but still struggle with the sin. He asked the Lord why He wouldn't set him free. The Lord said it was because he didn't hate the sin enough.

Jesus must come first if we want to follow and obey Him. This means leaving our former ways at the cross and daily choosing Him. We must encourage people to take on a healthy attitude and lifestyle in order to remain healed.

Repent and Start Again

The enemy may attack our minds and hearts with temptation or negative thoughts, or throw painful encounters our way. We are to recognize when this happens, so we don't allow him a foothold to the door of our soul.

It may be we have forgiven someone and the same person hurts us again. We can choose not to let resentment, anger and bitterness in our souls, but to forgive them again and pray a blessing on their lives. Or we can choose to let the enemy in and suffer with the emotional or physical symptoms as a consequence. We need to protect our hearts and minds from the attacks of the enemy in order to stay healed. We shouldn't beat ourselves for failing to keep the enemy out, but rather take action each time we let him in, by kicking him out again. This may take more than one doing until we are in a stronger position to keep him out. Once we have overcome the enemy and no longer let the ungodly spirit back in (be it fear, doubt, lust, unforgiveness etc.), then it is less likely to bother us. When the enemy realizes we are no longer influenced in this area, he will stop this method of attack and try another. That is his nature.

Sometimes, an area may require further ministry to address possible deeper roots. We may have had some branches removed but not tackled the main root.

Having a negative thought or being tempted isn't necessary a sin, but what we then do with the thought can make it sin. For example, I may have an ungodly or negative thought about someone, but if I choose to ignore it or replace it with a godly thought, then I haven't allowed it in. The enemy will throw all sorts of negative thoughts and temptations at us about others and ourselves. We mustn't spiral down with them by entertaining them, but instead stop thinking like that, rebuke the thoughts and think in the opposite spirit and mindset. It can be compared to getting dirt on our lenses. The lenses represent the window to our soul. We can wash off the dirt with the cleansing water of the Holy Spirit, instead of allowing the dirt to block the way we see or think.

A lady had inflammatory bowel disease as a result of harbouring feelings such as anger, unforgiveness and resentment. After dealing with these emotions, her symptoms got better and her bowel recovered. Sometime later, new issues arose causing her again to respond with negative feelings. Sure enough, her bowel symptoms returned. Again, after dealing with these negative thoughts, her bowel improved.

Standing Firm on the Truth

Paul tells us to pray in the Spirit on all occasions so we may keep our minds alert from the fiery darts of the enemy (Ephesians 6:18, Philippians 4:8). Sometimes, the enemy throws the symptoms back at us and tells us we haven't been healed. If we believe the lie that we haven't been healed, then the sickness will return. However, if we stand firm on the truth and word of God that we have been healed, the symptoms will flee.

We are not to be discouraged if symptoms return after receiving healing, but recognize this as a need to take spiritual authority over the symptoms again. It is not right to think that because the symptoms have returned we haven't been healed. Rather, we should stand firm in the faith that we have been healed, and command the symptoms to leave. I have met people who have been healed from cancer of the bowel and Crohn's disease, only for their symptoms to come back at a later date.

However, when they have stood on the word that they were healed, their symptoms disappeared over the following days or weeks.

Renewing the Mind

After people are freed from fears, lies or false beliefs, then new pathways need to form in their thought pattern or belief system. This is done through renewing the mind by regularly declaring God's truths.

New thought patterns develop when we proclaim the truths on a regular basis for at least three weeks. Scientific studies have shown it takes around three weeks or more for a new neuronal or thought pathway to develop in the brain, as long as it is nurtured on a regular basis. This is known as *neuroplasticity*. For example, I may have struggled with the lie that God doesn't have time to listen to me, or I'm not good enough. Yet, if I replace this with Holy Spirit truth (such as, He wants to speak to me and is there for me every moment of the day, or the truth I am wonderfully made), then my brain will develop this new belief pattern as new 'wires' or neurones begin to form. Whatever we feed to our thoughts will start to grow, whether good or bad. And what we stop thinking (or no longer feed) can become redundant.

Creating new pathways in our brain is a bit like driving a car across a field full of tall grass. We can choose to create a new path across the grass instead of driving down the old established path. By repeatedly driving along the new route, a path will begin to form. Likewise, by no longer driving along the old path, the route will become redundant as the grass grows again making the old path no longer visible. This applies to rewiring the brain as we choose to believe in God's word and truth, and stop entertaining the lies and fears of the enemy.

Renewing the mind is about replacing our old negative thoughts (or toxic thoughts) with a Kingdom mindset, as God reveals His truths in exchange for each fear and lie. This rewiring may take time until the new thought patterns have been established.

Worship & Pray in Tongues

One of the ways to stay healed is to regularly pray and worship, through giving thanks and praise. Thanks and praise can release healing and keep us healthy. The leper who returned to Jesus with thanks and praise, stayed healed.

Praying in tongues is a powerful gift of warfare. We are encouraged to pray in the Spirit on *all* occasions and not just when we feel like it (Ephesians 6:18). Praying in tongues helps us to pray in the Spirit instead of the flesh. We are to pray for His will to be done, instead of ours. When we are struggling to pray in our natural language, we can always pray in our spiritual language. *'We do not know what we ought to pray for, but the Spirit Himself intercedes for us with groans that words can't express'* (Romans 8:26).

He has given us the gift of praying in tongues, which is a prayer language in the Spirit. I don't understand it, but He does. The enemy is barred from knowing what conversation I am having with God for it is Spirit to spirit, hence it is powerful. Sometimes the tongue language may be in another known language (like when the disciples spoke in different tongues on the day of Pentecost), or it may be in a supernatural language that only God and His angels understand. *'For anyone who speaks in a tongue doesn't speak to men but to God. Indeed no-one understands him; he utters mysteries with his spirit'* (1 Corinthians 14:2-3).

Many times I find myself praying first in my spiritual language then in my natural. The two go hand-in-hand, especially when interceding or praying for someone. Paul encourages us to pray with our spirit and then with our mind (1 Corinthians 14:15). Praying in tongues is edifying for ourselves. It is a powerful tool to connect us to the Spirit of God. *'But you, dear friends, **build yourselves up** in your most holy faith and **pray in the Holy Spirit'*** (Jude 1:20). When others have asked me to pray for specific areas or healing, I have first prayed in tongues. This has enabled me to be led by the Spirit regarding how to pray.

The gift of tongues is powerful when used for personal prayer and worship as well as corporate prayer and ministry. It is a powerful weapon in warfare prayer. Praying in tongues can build up our spirit, especially during dry seasons. Praying in the

Spirit also helps us when ministering to others. It is a powerful tool during intercessory prayer, since it breaks down enemy strongholds. Also, it is a necessary tool for our daily life.

Many credible prophets agree we should pray in tongues for at least an hour each day. There is power when we do this. Our flesh comes under our spirit, and our spirit submits to the reign of God's Spirit. This helps us keep more in tune with God's Spirit throughout the day. Apparently, there are studies which indicate that praying in tongues on a regular basis is beneficial to our health, especially our immune system.

These are some ways to staying healed instead of losing the healing. I encourage people to stay healed by simply making them aware of what may happen after the healing, and the ways to overcome.

Conclusion

When I started medical school, it took five years of training or 'preparation' before qualifying as a doctor. Those initial five years laid a foundation for my work in the medical healing profession. Though I started with little knowledge and skills, I was able to build upon this foundation with further training and experience.

The main foundation for healing in the Kingdom is an intimate relationship with God. We can only serve in the Kingdom if we know the King Himself. Upon this foundation, we can discover ways to minister freedom and healing, both on an individual and corporate level, as we co-labour with His Spirit.

The foundation for a building usually consists of a mixture of cement and stones. The stones are like the teaching and training on healing, and the cement is like our relationship with God. Without the cement, the stones would crumble or fall away. Hence, both are required, though the cement is the vital ingredient to provide a firm foundation on which to build. Unless the Lord builds the house its builders labour in vain (Psalm 127:1).

Likewise, an operating room has to be prepared for every surgical procedure, with the appropriate tools for each operation. Hence, this leads us to Volume 2, *Kingdom Tools*. Kingdom Tools reveals ways to use and apply the various spiritual tools for the different areas of healing. Having a spiritual foundation enables us to use these tools with greater efficacy, as we discover how to co-labour with the Great Physician, Jesus.

RECOMMENDED FURTHER READING

Mahesh Chavda: *Hidden Power of Prayer and Fasting*
T.L Osborn: *Healing the Sick*
Bill Johnson & Randy Clark: *Essential Guide to Healing*
Henry Wright: *A More Excellent Way*
Heidi Baker: *Birthing the Miraculous*
Dawna Desilva &Teresa Liebscher: *Sozo*
Chester & Betsy Kylstra: *Biblical Healing & Deliverance*
John G Lake: *His Life, His Sermons, His Boldness of Faith*
Arthur Burk: *Blessing Your Spirit*
Dr Caroline Leaf: *Who Switched off my Brain*
Benny Hinn: *The Blood*
Mahesh Chavda: *The Hidden Power of the Blood of Jesus*
Benny Johnson: *Power of the Blood*
Wendy Alec: *Visions from Heaven*
Joyce Meyer: *The Battle Belongs to the Lord*
Tony Stoltzfus: *The Calling Journey*
Mark Nysewander: *The Fasting Key*
Francis Macnutt: *Healing*
James Goll: *The Lost Art of Practicing His Presence*
John Eckhardt: *Deliverance and Spiritual warfare*
Bill Johnson: *Supernatural Power of a Transformed Mind*
John & Mark Sandford: *Deliverance and Inner Healing*
Neil Anderson: *Freedom In Christ*
Pablo Bottari: *Free in Christ*
Joan Hunter: *Freedom Beyond Comprehension*
Roberts Liardon: *John G Lake on Healing*
Roberts Liardon: *God's Generals- The Healing Evangelists*
Morris Cerullo: *Demolishing Demonic Strongholds*
Don Basham: *Deliver Us From Evil*
A.W Tozer: *Pursuit of God*
Kathie Walters: *Spirit of False Judgement*
Richard Ing: *Waging Spiritual Warfare*
Andrew Murray: *Humility*
Mark Virkler: *How to hear God's voice*
John Paul Jackson: *The Art of Hearing God*

Appendix A

Ungodly Strongholds

Here are some examples of how ungodly strongholds may have various branches or ungodly fruit. The list is not complete. Hence, we need to rely on the Holy Spirit to draw attention to the spiritual or emotional roots behind the fruit.

Unforgiveness
- *Resentful / jealous*
- *Anger/ Revenge*
- *Bitterness/ Judgment*
- *Fault-finding/ Complaining /Accusing*
- *Slander/ Criticism*
- *Hatred/ Blame*

Judgment
- *Pride of knowledge / Superiority*
- *Critical/ Faultfinding*
- *Accusing/Pointing the finger*
- *Jealous /Competitive / intimidating*
- *Racist / Miscommunication*

Anger
- *Unforgiveness*
- *Frustration*
- *Revenge/punishment*
- *Hatred/Violence/destruction*
- *Not listened to/ being misunderstood*
- *Rejection /abandonement*

Oppression
- *Lies/false beliefs/ negative thoughts*
- *People to forgive*
- *Things to repent (or wrong choices made)*

- *Self-pity*
- *Disappointment/ frustration*
- *Suicidal thoughts/ death/ depression*
- *Hopelessness/ despair/mistrust*

Rebellion

- *Independent spirit (do what you want)*
- *Pride & Superiority (pride of knowledge or status)*
- *Disobedience to God's will & others*
- *Stubbornness/ stiff necked*
- *Fear and control*
- *People need to forgive*

Competition

- *Striving/ Driven by selfish- ambition*
- *Jealousy*
- *Need for achievement or success*
- *Need to be recognised*
- *Need to be better than others*
- *Fear of failure/ insecure*
- *Need to be a perfectionist*

Abandonment/ Rejection

- *Loneliness /Isolation*
- *Fear of being alone*
- *Fear of not good enough/ not wanted/not liked*
- *Fear of man or fear of being rejected*
- *Not belonging*
- *Self-pity /competition*
- *Orphan spirit*
- *Perceived rejection (think rejected when actually not)*
- *Victim mindset/ Self-pity*

Sexual Sins

- *Adultery /soul-ties*
- *Masturbation/Pornography*

- *Incest/ Rape*
- *Abuse (to others or been abused)*
- *Abortion /premarital sex*
- *Bestiality*
- *Lust/Cravings/impure desires & thoughts*
- *Homosexuality/ Lesbianism*
- *Incubus/succubus/demonic sex*
- *Prostitution/ offering sex for gain*
- *Guilt & shame (may be false if been abused)*
- *Sense of Defilement /Feeling unclean*

Occult Involvement (list is huge, here are some)
- *Psychic readings/healing*
- *Palm readings /Tarot cards/Tea leave reading*
- *Seances/ clairvoyance/ Ouiji board/ Contacting ancestral spirits*
- *Astral Travel/Automatic writing*
- *False gifts (counterfeit healing, tongues, prophecy...)*
- *Freemasonry*
- *Fortune telling / Divination*
- *Mental Telepathy*
- *Transcendental Meditation/ Yoga*
- *Voodoo/Witchcraft (white, black or red)/Satanic worship*
- *Spells/sorcery/Spiritism/Water spirits*
- *Vampire / Werewolf*

Male /Female domination
- *Need for control*
- *Emotional manipulation*
- *Physical/verbal/sexual abuse*
- *Intimidation*
- *Bullying*
- *Jezebel spirit*
- *Pride /superiority*
- *Feminist/ Male Chauvinist/*
- *Freemasonry*

Freemasonry

The prayers can be found from the following sources;

a) For a summarized version: '*Unmasking Freemasonry, Removing the Hoodwink*' by Selwyn Stevens, published by Jubilee

b) For specific prayers relating to the higher degrees: '*Freemasonry: Death in the family*' by Yvonne Kitchen, published by Fruitfulvine Publishing House, (*www.fruitfulvine.com.au*)

Deception

- *Double-mindedness*
- *Unbelief/ scepticism*
- *Occult Involvement/ witchcraft*
- *Lying /Fraudulence*
- *Secretive/ hiddenness*
- *Self-deception (unaware lying)*
- *Mind blocking*
- *Delusion / Confusion*
- *Need to over justify*

Pride

- *Self-centredness/ Self-importance*
- *Superiority/ Self-righteous/ concerned about reputation*
- *Always right/ Self-opinionated*
- *Self-ambition/ Vanity*
- *Racism/ cultural superiority*
- *False humility / pretense*
- *Sarcasm/ ridicule / mocking*
- *Pride of knowledge/ Pride of achievement /pride of possessions*
- *Easily offended*

Shame

- *True shame (guilty of sin)/ False shame (projected by others)*
- *Volatile Anger/ Blame others*
- *Condemnation/ Not worthy to be forgiven /Can't forgive self*
- *Self-pity/ Victim mindset*
- *Abuse /Self-hate/ Self-rejection*
- *Embarrassment/Fear of what others think (shame/fear/control)*
- *Hopelessness/ Suicidal*

Fear/ Anxiety/Panic attacks

There are many fears not listed here. People can fear anything. This may be a result of past experience, what they have read or seen in social media, on the news or what they have heard others say or experience.

- *False responsibility*
- *Mistrust in God*
- *Fear of...? (no money, failure, rejection, sickness, death, attack...). Fears are linked to not feeling in control.*
- *Insecurity/ uncertainty*
- *Tiredness/exhaustion / confusion*
- *Lies/False beliefs (False Evidence Appearing Real)*
- *Insomnia / witchcraft*
- *Generational (anxiety & fears passed down the blood line).*

Alternative Medicines

There are many not listed here, and this is just some.

- *Hypnosis*
- *Reflexology*
- *Homeopathy*
- *Acupuncture*
- *Reiki*
- *Traditional Chinese Medicine*
- *Chiropractice*
- *Tai Chi / Other Martial Arts*
- *Yoga*

Note: If a person has just one or two areas of ungodly fruit in each of the above categories, then the issue isn't necessarily a stronghold. Hence, these issues will have relatively shallow roots and therefore be easier to address. (They are more like plants instead of trees in our spiritual garden).

Appendix B

BY THE AUTHOR

Kingdom Medicine Volume Two provides a range of Kingdom Tools to assist in healing and freedom. The purpose of *Kingdom Tools* is to empower and equip the body of Christ with tools that can help identify the underlying issues, as well as provide ways to release healing and freedom.

Kingdom Medicine Volume Three looks at *Divine Heart Surgery.* This is advanced healing and requires coming into God's presence to assist the Great Surgeon operate on people's hearts. As we minister in His presence, we have the privilege of seeing what He does, as He delicately heals the wounded emotions and restores the traumatized areas of the heart. It involves additional tools including *Accessing the Courts of Heaven* and *Synchronising Areas of the Heart. (This will be available in 2021).*

Into His Chambers is based on a vision and invites you to come deeper into the heart of God by encountering the chambers of *Belonging, Identity, Suffering Heart of Christ* and *Anointing*. It is full of revelatory insight to help you go deeper in your relationship with God, including the power of His grace and the cross. It invites you to encounter His glory-presence in the Holy of Holies, and to become one who carries the heart of a prophet, priest, servant and king (2018).

Whilst Angela was ministering in the war-torn nation of South Sudan, the Lord spoke to her heart to prepare His warrior bride. This book is rich with scriptures, revelations and powerful testimonies to call forth His warriors and prepare His glorious bride for His return. (2016)

At the peak of her medical career, Angela had a call on her life to work amongst the poor in Africa. What she didn't know was that God was going to derail her and take her down an unfamiliar path. As she obeyed God's call, she discovered another realm to sickness and disease; a realm that wasn't found in medical textbooks. Instead she received "on the job training" from the Great Physician Himself. This book combines faith with medicine, the supernatural with the natural and the physical with the emotional and spiritual, as you read the powerful testimonies and teachings on how to heal the sick, God's way! (2014).

Appendix C

ABOUT THE AUTHOR

Angela Walker qualified as a doctor at Liverpool Medical School in 1991 and went on to pursue a career in Paediatrics and Child Health at the London teaching hospitals. She furthered her studies by taking a Master's degree in Clinical Paediatrics, followed by a Diploma in Tropical Medicine and Hygiene, before she went and served with Voluntary Services Oversees as a Paediatric lecturer in Uganda.

After becoming a Consultant in 2004, she studied at All Nations Bible College in Hertfordshire. Following this, she served with Iris Global for seven years on the mission field in Africa, where she practiced Kingdom Medicine. During this time, she discovered the possibility of there being spiritual and emotional roots to sickness and disease, and this prompted her to write her first book, 'Healing God's Way'.

She is an inspirational speaker, trainer, and pioneer with a passion to see hearts restored, people set free, lives transformed and God's Kingdom advance in the nations. She is the founder and director of THEO Ministries.

For further copies of her books, invitations to speak or any other enquiries, please visit the web or email:

www.theoministries.com
info@theoministries.com

Printed in Great Britain
by Amazon

62495441R00119